BIGOTRY

Kathlyn Gay

ENSLOW PUBLISHERS, INC.

Bloy St. & Ramsey Ave.   P.O. Box 38
Box 777   Aldershot
Hillside, N.J. 07205   Hants GU12 6BP
U.S.A.   U.K.

Library of Congress Cataloging in Publication Data

Gay, Kathlyn
  Bigotry.

  Bibliography: p.
  Includes index.
  Summary: Traces the history of various forms of bigotry,
the effects it has on society, and ways of combating it.
    1. United States–Race relations–Juvenile literature.
2. Racism–United States–Juvenile literature.
3. Prejudices–United States–Juvenile literature.
4. Civil rights–United States–Juvenile literature.
[1. Race relations. 2. Racism. 3. Prejudices.
4. Civil rights] I. Title.
E184.A1G33   1989   305.8'00973   88-30428
ISBN 0-89490-171-0

Printed in the United States of America

10 9 8 7 6 5 4 3 2

Illustration Credits:
Courtesy of: American-Arab Anti-Discrimination Committee, p. 32;
AP/Wide World Photos, pp. 20, 58, 66, 76; Kathlyn Gay, pp.
8, 90, 118; Klanwatch, p. 44; Milwaukee Committee on
Community Relations, p. 106.

BIGOTRY

For Marla and Dana, who so diligently monitored news sources for reports of ethnoviolence and other racist and bigoted acts in their particular regions of the nation.

Acknowledgments

Many people were very helpful in providing reports and other materials describing bigoted and racist acts and ways to overcome such behavior. I especially appreciate the efforts of Frances M. Sonnenschein, Director National Education Department of the Anti-Defamation League of B'nai B'rith; Norman L. Gissel, Kootenai County Task Force on Human Relations; Joan C. Weiss, Executive Director National Institute Against Prejudice & Violence; Abdeen Jabara, President American-Arab Anti-Discrimination Committee; Bridget Bannon, Executive Director, Milwaukee Commission on Community Relations; Leonard Jarzab, President Polish-American Guardian Society; Julian Johnson, Director of Development Legal Defense Fund NAACP; Frederick D. Wright, Assistant Dean and Director Black Studies Program, University of Notre Dame; Janet Himler, Assistant Regional Director ADL of Los Angeles; staffs of the National Urban League, the Klanwatch project of the Southern Poverty Law Center (Montgomery, Alabama), Ventura County (California) Historical Society, Council on Interracial Books for Children, Inc. (New York City).

–Kathlyn Gay

Contents

Report cites misery for blacks

Says no progress made in Reagan years

Black claims police brutality

School buildings defaced with white-power slogans

radio sports announcer in the 1940s he editorialized that blacks should be allowed to play major ___ baseball. This is the ___ man who has been ___ United State ___ offer?

___ about the criticisms leveled at him by various black civil rights leaders, Reagan responded by saying, "Some of those leaders are doing very well leading organizations based on keeping alive the feeling that they're victims of prejudice."

This comment, keep in ___ was offered just a few ___ ther King ___ whi ___

MINORITIE

versy

Varying Dress, Idioms

'Jew' as slur sparks cont___

Races Split by 'Cultural Divide'

Oxf___ compromise fails to end ___ Act.

Rioting er___ in Mi___ after black killed

Latinos Face Another 'Hard Decade,'

White supremacists muster 6

DAY 3 OF A 5-PART SERIES:
Black professionals talk about their lives in a community that does not reflect their heritage,

done was ___ the statistical reports that ___ ent has been ___ lag

incom___ ___n. The rate ___ ___nortality, drug a___ ___ infection, teen-age ___ single-parenthood ks is far above that of at large. Certainly the ___n't believe that's all by ___ accident. ___tressing of all about ___sponse is that his inter- ___ giving him an exit ___o defend his ad___ ___rd ___ ___p

sponsi___ of certain ___ called attention ___ where his record has be___ of accomplishment. History ___ or may not be kind to ___ Reagan in asse___ the ___

An officer fired ___t the ___ ___ds

Middle-class residents face racis___

integration plan *Memories of King feed desire to help city needy*

Court deals blow to minority hiring

Stereotypes Magnified

Minorities in TV: Black, White Issue

Bigotry, racism, discrimination . . . everywhere.

1

What's a Bigot?
Who's a Racist?

In our neighborhood there are mostly white people, except for a family from India. But last week a young black couple was looking at a house for rent across the street from us. I thought my dad would go crazy. He went right out to talk to some of our neighbors, trying to get them all worked up so they'd protest to the owner about renting to black people. Look. I love my dad, but he was wrong to do what he did. How could he know what that couple is like? None of us will know because they didn't rent the house. I hope it wasn't because of my dad or our neighbors, but I have a feeling it was.

C.S., Elkhart, Indiana

A bunch of us went into this video store the other day. We were just going to rent a movie. But this old guy who owns the place kept glaring at us and started following us around. We got pissed and left. What is it about old people? Do they think all kids steal or what?

Brad, Denver, Colorado

I thought I was prepared when I went to this new high school. I know that other people think I'm strange, with my short arms and legs, but I've learned to accept my "problem." It's called achondroplasia—or dwarfism. Over the years I've gotten used to nicknames like Shrimp and Small Fry, but this boy really threw me. He came up to me in the hall and asked, "When you going to join the circus?" I was upset all day. Just because I'm different doesn't mean I'm a freak!

J.M., Waukegan, Illinois

I volunteered to do this project, but the morning I was supposed to go to class all dressed up like a "bag lady" I got scared. Like my stomach was all jumpy and I didn't know if I wanted to go through with it. The social studies teacher had asked for someone to come to school looking very different from everyone else. Then the rest of the class was supposed to tell what they thought of the person. Well, I knew everybody would have a lot of bad things to say. They wouldn't really be talking about me, but, well, I was inside the clothes and, I don't know, it made me feel out of place!

Nissa, Ventura, California

At first it was just teasing—kids are into that, so it didn't bother me too much. But then it became a daily thing. When my younger sister goes to school with me, I always hold her hand so the kids call us "lezzies." It hurts because my sister is blind. Most of the time she does very well on her own, but sometimes she needs my help. Why don't other people understand that? Why do they have to be so mean?

Betterae, South Bend, Indiana

That last question is one that is often raised by people who have been victims of others' prejudices, or prejudgments. *Prejudice* literally means "judging beforehand without knowledge or examination of the facts," or strongly holding a preconceived notion, idea, or attitudes.

However, prejudgment does not necessarily mean that a person forms an adverse or negative opinion about something or someone. It is possible to have a prejudice, or bias, *for* something—such as a certain type of food or make of car. Many people, for example, have preconceived ideas that democracy is valuable and that democratic rule is a fair form of government. More often, though, and in the context of this book, *prejudice* is used to mean unfavorably prejudging others without reason and with misinformation.

Prejudiced people are likely to act in ways that can harm those they judge in a negative manner, as the brief comments at the beginning of this chapter point out. In fact, many prejudiced people might also be called bigots. According to one simple definition, a bigot is a person who is stubbornly and unreasonably attached to an opinion or belief. You might, for example, hear a bigot argue, "The world is flat—that's what I was taught and that's what I believe. Period." You could pull out maps and globes and call attention to geographic explanations about the shape of the earth. But scientific information would not convince someone attached to a flat-earth theory to change her or his mind.

Usually, acting on prejudiced notions, bigoted people are intolerant of those who differ from them in color or national ancestry, or in religious or political beliefs. In the popular TV show of the 1960s *All in the Family*, the not-too-bright character Archie Bunker was the prime example of a bigoted person. Not only was he stubbornly attached to the "rightness" of his point of view whatever that might be. He also acted out his intolerance by insulting people who had political or religious affiliations different from his own. Or he expressed his dislike for and even hatred of those who were not part of his in-group.

Many of Archie Bunker's antics were considered humorous because his bigotry was depicted as absurd, if not downright silly. At the time it seemed that Archie's actions did not seriously hurt anyone but him. However, critics of the show have argued that this portrayal of Archie Bunker made it seem "normal" or acceptable to be a bigot, glossing over the fact that bigotry frequently has an ugly and virulent side.

Bigotry and prejudice quite often lead to stereotypes, or fixed ideas about a particular group. People are seen as part of a group rather than being recognized as individuals. Those who accept stereotypes about groups different from them might express those attitudes in statements like these:

Older people are crotchety.
Young people are selfish.
Boys are mean.
Girls are silly.
Asians are sneaky.
Native Americans are alcoholics.
Blacks are lazy.
Arabs are terrorists.
Hispanics are hot-tempered.
Lawyers are greedy.
Artists are unreliable.

Many stereotypes are fabrications, made up to show a group in an unfavorable way. Some stereotypes are based on an element of truth that is exaggerated. In other words, a few people in a group may have certain traits that are considered negative. But those selected traits certainly do not describe all people in a group and do not give a full picture of any one person in a group. Stereotypes, in short, ignore variations in people. So, if you have a stereotype idea about a group of people, you easily can overlook and never get to know what individuals within a group are really like.

Stereotypes are often the basis for discrimination, in which people who are members of a stereotyped group are excluded from jobs, housing, schools, and other institutions. In a recent case, a young black woman involved in a University of Georgia on-the-job training program was hired to be a pharmacist's assistant in a Tifton, Georgia, drugstore. But the white owner of the store fired the young woman because he said "customers complained" about being waited on by a black person. Many Tifton residents denied this was true, but the pharmacist believed his customers would not accept the black woman as an individual but would see her only as part of a group that had been judged "inferior." The pharmacist may have been acting on his own stereotypical view, passing judgment based on preconceived notions.

Victims of stereotypes may also become scapegoats, or targets for blame. American Arabs, for example, have been subjected to hostile attacks. Attackers blame all Middle East problems on people of Arab ancestry.

Scapegoating frequently involves bigoted rhetoric such as that used by Louis Farrakhan, a Black Muslim leader. Farrakhan continually blames all whites("devils" he calls them) for problems blacks face, spouting a particular hatred for Jews who Farrakhan falsely claims have "a stranglehold on the government of the United States." In 1985, Farrakhan drew 25,000 people to New York's Madison Square Garden to bellow his bigoted belief that "Farrakhan is hated by the Jews! . . . But if you rise up to try to kill me, then Allah promises you that he will bring on this generation the blood of the righteous. All of you will be killed outright . . . . God [will] put you in the oven."

Along with verbal attacks, scapegoating may lead to vandalizing buildings and other structures. In Springfield, Illinois, insulting statements about blacks and slogans such as "white power" and "white power rules" were painted on the tomb of Abraham Lincoln. Vandals used similar tactics to deface synagogues in many cities across the nation, scrawling anti-Semitic (anti-Jewish) statements on the buildings.

People exhibit their prejudices and bigotry in a variety of ways. In one incident, an Amish family, members of a religious group that shuns modern conveniences, were riding in a horse-drawn buggy along an Indiana highway where they were jeered and stoned by a gang of young people out "joy-riding" in a car. One member of the Amish family was injured. But the only comment afterward from a parent of one of the joy-riders was "boys will be boys."

Another incident took place in Los Angeles, where an inter-racial couple was forced to leave their $135,000 home in a predominantly white neighborhood. Shortly after moving in, the couple, a black man and a white woman, received racist leaflets and hate mail saying "blacks are trash" and "the zoo wants you." Continued harassment drove the couple out.

In Yonkers, New York, several city council members refused to obey a federal court order to build low-income housing units in predominantly white neighborhoods. The U.S. district judge fined the city and its officials and noted that for forty years Yonkers officials had deliberately placed federally subsidized apartments in black neighborhoods only. Since many blacks and other minorities have lower incomes than whites, the assumption was that only minorities would use subsidized housing. By keeping low-income housing out of white neighborhoods, segregated housing patterns have been maintained not only in Yonkers, but also in many other U.S. cities. Certainly there are integrated communities across the nation, but race often determines whether a person can get a home mortgage, and real estate agents tend to steer black or other minority buyers away from white neighborhoods.

In a suburb of New Orleans, Sheriff Harry Lee ordered his deputies to routinely stop blacks who happened to be driving through white neighborhoods. His orders were part of a plan to cut down on home burglaries, and he reportedly said that blacks traveling through all-white neighborhoods were "up to no good." Lee's remarks and actions brought sharp criticism from the president of the New Orleans chapter of the National Association for the Advancement of Colored People (NAACP), and Lee publicly apologized to the black community. Lee, of Chinese ancestry, denied he is prejudiced, saying he has often been the victim of prejudice himself.

In Philadelphia, Boston, Washington, D.C., Los Angeles, and many other U.S. cities, Asian immigrants—Vietnamese, Koreans, Cambodians, Laotians—have been insulted, attacked, and had their property vandalized by blacks and whites who resent their presence. Gangs in New Jersey, who brag that they are "dot busters," have attacked people from India, labeling them "dot heads" because of the red markings women wear on their foreheads.

In Howard Beach, a white ethnic neighborhood of Queens, New York, a gang of youths attacked several black men, chasing them from the area with the cry "Niggers, get out!" One black man was beaten with a tire iron and broom handles. The black youth was chased onto a highway, where he was struck by a car and killed. Three of the white youths were convicted of manslaughter.

Not long after the Howard Beach incident, a gang of black youths in Brooklyn, New York, attacked a white youth out for a walk with two friends. The gang of young blacks apparently wanted to retaliate for "white racism."

Although most scientists today reject the idea of categorizing people according to race—that is, creating terms for subspecies of *Homo sapiens*—race is used to define people in social terms. *Racism,* then, refers to a form of prejudice in

15

which members of a group (determined by physical characteristics) believe they are superior to all other groups of people.

On a national scale, racism can be institutionalized. In other words, the majority of people in a nation may feel it is "right" or acceptable to have unfavorable stereotypes of and prejudice against certain groups, particularly religious and racial or, more correctly, ethnic groups (those who share a culture different from the majority way of life). When those unfavorable opinions become institutionalized, widespread discrimination results.

During World War II, for example, American citizens of Japanese descent who lived on the west coast of the United States were herded up and sent to inland relocation camps. Why? Because Japan had just bombed Pearl Harbor, an American military base in the Pacific. Secretary of War Henry L. Stimson wrote in a memorandum to the president, "The Japanese race is an enemy race and while many second and third generation Japanese born on United States soil, possessed of United States citizenship, have become 'Americanized,' the racial strains are undiluted." Thus, the secretary of war assumed that American citizens of Japanese ancestry would "turn against this nation when the final test of loyalty comes." He acknowledged that there had been no acts of disloyalty but, he wrote, "The very fact that no sabotage has taken place is a disturbing and confirming indication that such action will be taken."

Such twisted reasoning—shared by many Americans at that time—convinced President Franklin D. Roosevelt to issue an executive order that authorized the secretary of war to set up military camps to hold people of Japanese ancestry. Clearly, this was a discriminatory act. The United States was also at war with Germany and Italy. Hundreds of thousands of people of German and Italian descent lived in every part of the nation.

But Americans of German and Italian ancestry were not singled out as "enemies" simply because of their heritage.

In spite of proven dedication to their country in the U.S. military and in civilian life, thousands of U.S. citizens of Japanese descent lost their land, businesses, homes, and personal property. They were "tagged" like so much baggage and sent to camps surrounded by barbed wire and guarded by the military. After the war, the federal government made some payments to American Japanese who lost property, but many claims were denied on the grounds that the military had acted out of necessity (which was later proven false).

Thirty-four years later, President Gerald Ford said, "We know now what we should have known then . . . . Japanese Americans were and are loyal Americans" both in battle and at home. In 1976, Ford terminated Roosevelt's executive order, which had never been formally rescinded, against American citizens of Japanese descent.

Finally, in September 1987 Congress approved a bill that provided for a token payment—a symbolic gesture, as it was called—of $20,000 each to more than 60,000 survivors of the relocation camps. Congress also set up a fund to be used to educate the public about the internment and included an apology in the bill, which stated that "a grave injustice was done to both citizens and permanent resident aliens of Japanese ancestry by the evacuation, relocation and internment of civilians during World War II. On behalf of the Nation, the Congress apologizes."

Yet other racist and bigoted acts continued to occur. Victims of bigotry have included not only racial and religious groups but also homosexuals, the poor, handicapped people and women. New victims of prejudice may appear at any time. For example, widespread fear about the AIDS epidemic has

17

prompted people to bar children who are AIDS victims from schools or to harass and discriminate against adults with AIDS.

Can anything be done to stop harassment and violence against people simply because of their physical handicaps, color, national background, religious preference, economic status, gender, or sexual orientation? Can prejudice be reduced? How can you counter stereotypes?

There are no simple answers. But the questions represent problems in human relations that many individuals and groups have been struggling with for decades, particularly in the United States, which is home for people from almost every ethnic, racial, and religious group in the world. To explore prejudiced attitudes and behavior, one needs to look first at the roots of bigotry and racism.

*The swastika, once the symbol of Nazi Germany, is now
used to promote hatred against many people.*

2

Why Bigotry and Racism?

Since the beginning of civilization, people within a common culture have been divided by class or caste with roles determined by their places in society. In the caste system of the ancient Greeks, only landowners could be citizens and they often spent their days in study and discussions. Slaves, who included conquered peoples as well as Greeks who could not pay their debts, provided labor for daily tasks.

Later, in feudal societies, people were divided into distinct classes. Merchants, commoners, and slaves were on the lowest rungs of the social ladder. They were expected to provide food, shelter, clothing, weapons, and other needed items for the knights, lords, and the king.

Whatever the division within a society, people were nevertheless bonded by common customs and language. It was not unusual to believe that one's own ethnic, or cultural, group was better than others. This belief, known as *ethnocentrism,* prompted the ancient Chinese, for example, to claim they were unique among early civilizations. Anyone who did not speak their language was considered a barbarian. Outsiders, even conquerors, were expected to adopt Chinese customs.

Throughout history, many groups of people have claimed superiority over other cultures and have labeled strangers barbarians, which often meant simply not being part of the ingroup. Some civilizations, such as the ancient Egyptians, considered themselves "more human" than any foreigners they encountered. Romans who conquered Greece believed they were far superior to those they ruled. Most conquerors, in fact, have believed that their ways were best.

Ethnocentrism frequently results in racial prejudice. But early civilizations seldom made distinctions on the basis of race, as the noted anthropologist Ashley Montagu pointed out in a classic work, *Man's Most Dangerous Myth: The Fallacy of Race*. People in earlier times were persecuted or discriminated against because of religious, cultural, political, or class differences, "but never on any biological grounds such as are implied in the idea of 'racial' differences . . . . The objection to any people on 'racial' or biological grounds is virtually a purely modern innovation," Montagu wrote.

Montagu and other anthropologists, along with many experts on human behavior, have stressed that great harm has been done by arbitrarily categorizing human populations by race. This does not mean the experts deny the physical differences in people, such as skin color, shape of the eyes, hair texture, and body structure. Rather, they note that along with the many variations in people, there are also basic similarities. The point is that exaggerating differences has led to a belief that there is a natural hierarchy of races, with some groups said to be more spiritually and mentally "advanced" than others.

Thus, it seems necessary to repeat and emphasize that the vast majority of scientists worldwide do not accept the concept that some groups are biologically superior to others. But

22

during Europe's "Age of Exploration," the racist view of white supremacy became firmly established among people of the so-called white races.

From the 1400s through the 1600s, explorers and conquerors from Europe returned home with vivid descriptions of Asians, Africans, and Native Americans, whom they called Indians. Most of the descriptions clearly showed that light-skinned Europeans had low regard and often hatred for people who had different shades of skin color, customs, languages, and clothing styles. Frequently Africans and Native Americans were referred to as "savages" and thought to be "subhumans."

Of all the physical characteristics, differences in skin color probably had the most impact on how Europeans viewed other groups. No one is sure why individuals have certain reactions to color, but many people have viewed dark colors in a negative manner. The color black, especially, is associated with such negatives as uncleanliness, evil, and death.

In themselves, negative color connotations would not be enough to keep racial bigotry alive and flourishing. But "scientific racism" attempted to give credence to the idea that certain races were inferior. Scientists based their theories on their own views of white supremacy. For example, some scientists believed that different races came from different origins and that only the light-skinned races made significant advances while others remained at "primitive" stages.

In the 1700s, a Swedish biologist, Carl Linnaeus, published his *Systema Naturae,* which categorized animals by Latin names and included in the animal kingdom *Homo sapiens,* or human. According to Linnaeus's view, all humans belonged to the same species subdivided into four races called *Homo sapiens americanus, Homo sapiens europaeus, Homo sapiens asiaticus,* and *Homo sapiens afer.*

Under each heading Linnaeus listed a variety of characteristics that in his view distinguished one race from another. Skin color was one distinguishing characteristic listed. Others included judgmental statements about a particular race, with the "red" group called "Resolute, cheerful, free," the "white" group called "Nimble, of the keenest mind," the "pale yellow" group called "Grave, proud, greedy," and the "black" group called "Cunning, lazy, careless."

After Charles Darwin's theory of evolution was published, a number of European and American intellectuals accepted the idea that humans originated from one source. But they used Darwin's ideas on natural selection to explain social order. Generally, natural selection is the concept that plants and animals respond to changes in the environment (such as climate) by inheritable adaptations or variations that take place over generations. If living things do not inherit characteristics that help them adapt, they die off.

A variety of factors affect how people develop and change, such as mutations (changes in genes), racial mixing, and migrations of people. But some scientists believe that natural selection has helped various groups survive. Differences in skin color, for example, might be one way that groups have adapted to climate changes. Dark skin contains large amounts of the pigment melanin, which helps protect the body from ultraviolet rays of the sun. So dark skin might have helped people survive in areas with much sunshine and high temperatures. People who migrated to areas with less sun may have developed lighter skin as an adaptation.

Another type of adaptation occurs in cold climate. People such as Eskimos have heavy-set bodies that tend to hold heat better than people who have tall, slender bodies.

Racists, however, have used the natural selection process to "prove" that a group's achievements are possible because of

24

heredity. In other words, light-skinned people interpreted Darwin's theory to mean that the white race had inherited traits that helped them accomplish more than darker races. Thus, light-skinned people were thought to be higher on the evolutionary ladder. Darker-skinned races were said to be the link closest to animals. Such a theory ignored or made light of achievements in many different cultures and the fact that the physical environment, education, wealth or lack of it, and other factors help determine what accomplishments a group will make.

By accepting a white supremacist view, light-skinned people could rationalize and justify subordinating darker-skinned peoples. In fact, European conquerors and colonists did just that. They claimed land and grabbed mineral wealth while forcing original populations in South America into slave labor and killing off thousands of Indians in both North and South America. In the process of establishing colonies, Europeans also exploited countless people in Asia and Africa, and they captured millions of Africans to be sold into slavery.

At the same time, Christianity played a role in reinforcing racist ideas. Many, but by no means all, Christian leaders in Europe and in the American colonies believed that Africans and Native Americans were "filthy pagans" and were not fit for anything except serving "superior" whites. That view, along with various aspects of scientific racism, became strongly entrenched, primarily because colonists needed labor to develop the land and build towns and cities. Since they could justify slavery on the basis of the victims' "subhuman" status, many early settlers adamantly defended slave trade. Some were even convinced that slavery would help bring salvation to the "heathens" and the slaves were "happy" because they had been "rescued from barbarism" and were provided with food and shelter. The fact that Africans lived in well-developed agricultural societies meant little or nothing to slave captors.

Ethnocentrism remained strong among the early colonists during the 1700s. The vast majority were white Anglo-Saxon Protestants (WASPs) from Britain and other northern European countries. They wanted to maintain the way of life they had known in their homelands, even though many eventually rebelled against English rule and fought for an independent nation. As John Jay noted in *The Federalist Papers* (written to explain the new Constitution of the United States), the people of the proposed new nation were a "united people—a people descended from the same ancestors, speaking the same language, professing the same religion, attached to the same principles of government, very similar in their manners and customs."

Although "professing the same religion," Protestant groups in the colonies were diverse in their beliefs and often in conflict. However, they were united in their prejudice against the Roman Catholic minority. In Maryland, for example, Catholics were denied political rights and were forbidden to hold religious services in public. Colonists also discriminated against Jews, barring them from voting in most colonies.

With the development of the new nation and the industrial revolution that followed, more and more people were needed to populate the land and to work in the fields and factories. By the mid-1800s, there was a great influx of newcomers. Most were WASPs from northern and western Europe, but a large percentage were Catholic immigrants from Germany and Ireland.

Even though the Germans and Irish were needed for the work force, they were not warmly greeted. Native-born Americans, or nativists as they were called, believed "alien riffraff" would take over and pollute their "pure native stock."

Then the nation would no longer be predominantly Anglo-Saxon.

Nativists resented the Germans and Irish for their clannishness and for preserving their Old World customs. Critics of the newcomers also argued that crime was on the increase and that immigrants overcrowded cities and produced slums. The Irish were especially scorned because of their poverty and what many nativists believed were boisterous drinking habits. There were fears as well that the Irish would take over jobs. Many factory and shop owners hung out signs saying, "No Irish Need Apply."

Nativism—sometimes described as a form of racism and certainly a display of ethnocentrism—was widespread among WASPs. Nativists called for restrictions on immigration, wrote books and pamphlets urging Protestants to fight the "Catholic menace," and incited anti-Catholic riots. Secret nativist societies sprang up, and eventually a national organization called the Supreme Order of the Star-Spangled Banner was formed. Members swore to secrecy and when asked about their activities would say, "I know nothing," earning them the name "Know-Nothings."

Eventually, the Know-Nothings formed a political party, but they gained little political strength. The party split over slavery. However, their anitforeignism flourished as immigrants continued to come from Europe, Asia, Mexico, and other parts of the world. Laws were passed to limit the number of some immigrant groups, such as the Chinese and Japanese, coming to the United States.

Many white Americans were particularly prejudiced against the Chinese and often brutally attacked Chinese immigrants. Newspapers carried highly charged editorials denouncing the Chinese as "inferior in most mental and bodily qualities." As one San Francisco editorial put it, the "Chinaman . . . is unable to communicate his ideas . . . is poor and mean, somewhat slavish and crouching, and is despised by the whites." Yet the whites eagerly recruited the Chinese to work for meager wages to develop agricultural lands and railroads. There is little doubt that the transcontinental railroad and western agricultural development in the United States depended on the underpaid, exploited labor of Chinese immigrants.

Historians have filled countless pages with stories about victims of nativism or antiforeignism, religious bigotry, and racism in the United States. But ethnocentrism has been as strong or stronger in other nations. A notorious example is the view held by Nazis in Germany during the 1930s and 1940s, the time of World War II.

Nazi leader Adolf Hitler claimed Aryans (meaning pureblooded gentile Germans) were the "superior race" and that "the purity of the German blood" had to be protected from Jews, whom Hitler labeled an "inferior race." The racist rhetoric prevailed in spite of the fact that superiority or inferiority is only in the eyes of the beholder and that biologically there is no such thing as a "Jewish race." People of many different national groups practice the religion and are part of the culture of Judaism.

However, Hitler's racism was accepted and acted upon. As is well known, the result was the Holocaust, one of the most repulsive mass murders in recent history—the killing of six million Jews and others who were considered "inferiors," such as gypsies and those who were mentally retarded, along with people who defied the Nazis in Germany and Nazi-occupied nations.

Racism has brought misery to millions of other people around the world. In South Africa, the system of apartheid keeps a small population of whites in power while relegating the great majority of the population who are blacks to low status and barring them from voting, jobs, adequate education, freedom of travel and the press, and other human rights.

Since ancient times, the Japanese have believed that their nation should be kept "ethnically pure" and that ethnic bonds, such as language, traditions, and religious practices, should be maintained. The Japanese are especially hard on minorities, who make up about 2 percent of the population. Koreans, the largest minority group, were forced to provide labor for the Japanese during and after World War II, and many Koreans in Japan today are denied citizenship and other privileges.

However, some Japanese appear to have even stronger feelings against blacks and Hispanics. In fact, in late 1986, Japan's prime minister, Yasuhiro Nakasone, said in a public speech that the reason Americans' intellectual achievements were lower than those of the Japanese was because "all those blacks, Puerto Ricans, and Mexicans are included." His statement shocked national leaders not only in the United States but also in some other nations of the world, and Nakasone eventually made a public apology.

In Britain, racism and "classism" have resulted in discrimination against black citizens who were recruited as laborers from former colonies in the Caribbean, Pakistan, and India. (All people of color in England are categorized as "black.") As British sociologist Michael Banton put it in a study of race and ethnicity in England, "The English do not draw a colour line as sharply as white Americans" but make distinctions on the basis of social status and economic class. Still, many Pakistanis and Indians do not describe themselves as black, believing it is a disparaging term, and separate themselves from Britons of Afro-Caribbean descent, whom whites relegate to the lowest status.

Although Afro-Caribbeans who have emigrated from formerly British colonies to England have the same citizenship rights as other Britons, they have suffered from white racism. An increasing number of blacks have been reporting verbal or physical assaults, and blacks as a group face an unemployment rate double that of the white population. With high unemployment since the 1960s, racism is especially hostile among whites who believe their joblessness is due to the recruitment of nonwhites. Yet immigration laws passed in the 1960s have sharply curtailed black immigration, and most black immigrants have been hired to do the dirty jobs that no one else would do.

On the North American continent, British Canadians, like Anglos in the United States, have long discriminated against the various Indian groups native to the land. As one scholar has pointed out, "Although their systems of government are quite different, both countries (Canada and the U.S.) developed land cession arrangements (or 'treaties') for displacing natives from valuable lands, and the subsequent development of reservations and reserves has perpetuated racial segregation . . . and lower class status for Indian people." The policy of both countries over the centuries has been to ignore the diversity of Native American societies and to see Indians as "childlike subordinates"—in short, "inferior" to the dominant societies of northern European ancestry.

Worldwide there have been attempts to improve relations between varied ethnic and national groups. Civil rights activists have helped bring about better treatment of those who have minority status in the United States. But attitudes toward minority groups (and women, who are a minority in economic and political power), are rooted in American history, and have helped keep racism and bigotry alive.

Stephen Steinberg, a U.S. sociology professor, summed it up in his book *The Ethnic Myth*. Nativists in the United States looked down upon European immigrants of the 1800s and thought their customs peculiar, but prejudice against European immigrants "was not as virulent, as pervasive, or as enduring as that experienced by racial minorities, nor was it given official sanction," Steinberg wrote. "When it came to racial minorities . . . the unspoken dictum was, 'No matter how much like us you are, you will remain apart.' Thus, at the same time that the nation pursued a policy aimed at the rapid assimilation of recent arrivals from Europe, it segregated the racial minorities." Although laws today prohibit various forms of segregation and discrimination, those practices still go on.

Stereotypes in the media can promote wrong ideas about some people and cultures.

3

What Keeps
Prejudice Alive?

In the United States, prejudice against certain groups of people has not remained static year after year. German, Irish, Scandinavian, and other European immigrants of the 1800s and 1900s became "Americanized" within two or three generations. Although they maintained much of their own cultures, the new Americans became part of what some historians have called a "Melting Pot" and others have referred to as a "Tossed Salad," here meaning a place where cultures are blended.

However, the very people who had earlier been the targets of prejudice often turned on later immigrants, particularly if they appeared different from the majority in skin color or were non-English-speaking, as were Hispanics. Racial minorities and some non-Christian groups already in the United States also continued to be set apart and were discriminated against in many other ways.

A variety of social, economic, and psychological factors have helped sustain racial prejudice and religious bigotry. In the first place, negative ideas about minority groups are often passed on from one generation to the next. For example, many

33

middle-class white children are brought up in neighborhoods or communities where they have little or no contact with people of color. Within such communities there may be a widespread belief that people of color are "inferior." Thus, children easily absorb such notions and assume they are factual rather than subjective judgments.

The community as a source of prejudice was clearly observed by young people at Glenbard East High School in a Chicago suburb. The Glenbard students put together a book titled *Teenagers Themselves,* which includes opinions on a variety of subjects from teenagers across the country. In a chapter called "Prejudice," the teenagers pointed out bigoted and racist attitudes in their families, neighbors, teachers, friends, and themselves. As the high school students responsible for compiling material for the book wrote, "Maybe it's too optimistic to hope that someday people will be judged as individuals. The disease [prejudice] would have to be stopped right at its source, the parents. Chances are, however, they'll find a cure for the common cold before they find a cure for prejudice."

Children learn at a young age how their families and friends view those who are considered "different" or "unacceptable." For example, parents or other adults might tell a child not to play with "those people." However, the term "those people" is usually replaced with such racial or ethnic slurs as "spics," "gooks," "greasy wops," "kikes," "desert niggers," or any number of other labels too numerous and not worth the space to list. The adults' words are reinforced with facial expressions and body gestures that clearly imply that "those people" are "inferior to *our* people." Some parents even punish their children if they associate with those who have been labeled "inferior."

Unfavorable images of various groups—including the handicapped and women—have been reinforced in books, newspapers, magazines, radio, TV, movies, and stage performances. People who are "dwarfed," for example, have been shown as "evil" or "bewitched." The physically disabled have been portrayed as "sinister." Girls and women have been stereotyped as "frail" and "emotional," or as "witches" and "bitches."

Stereotypes of ethnic groups have appeared in all the media. Italians, for example, have been shown as Mafia types, connected with crime and brutality. Swedes have been portrayed as "country bumpkins," Poles as "stupid," Irish as "foolish," and Mexicans as "lazy." The Chinese have been seen as "coolies"—railroad and laundry workers or house servants. Such stereotypes have prevailed as a way to keep people in "their place," and at various times in history have been a way to prevent groups from competing with the established majority for jobs and political power.

One negative image that was kept alive for many years was the view of the black male as a "Sambo" character, also known by such names as "Rastus" and "Uncle Remus." The black man was singled out to be the buffoon, with oversized lips lined with red, bulging eyes, always grinning broadly, dancing, singing, joking—or more frequently being the butt of jokes—looking and acting foolish for the entertainment of white folks. Such an image was rooted in slavery when black men, women, and children were expected to sing and dance as well as work for the white slave "masters." After slavery was abolished, the male Sambo character and his female counterpart, often known as "Aunt Jemima," appeared "in every nook and cranny of the popular culture," as historian Joseph Boskin put it.

In a study titled *Sambo: The Rise and Demise of an American Jester*, Boskin pointed out that making blacks appear foolish as well as forcing them to entertain was a way for whites to deny black men their manhood. Although the Sambo image began to fade in the 1930s, it was used until the 1960s in printed materials ranging from newspapers to brochures. It was also pictured on products such as postcards, children's games and books, posters, playing cards, sheet music covers, food packages, placemats, pillows, goblets, and tea sets.

Countless Sambo figures appeared as iron jockeys on front lawns or as ceramic figurines for indoor "decorations." The Sambo figure was found in most types of performances—skits, musicals, circuses, radio and TV shows, and even in parades. And, as Boskin wrote, "Sambo's happy, grinning countenance lit up restaurants, stores, hotels, businesses, universities, and even churches."

With Sambo shown everywhere as the foolish clown, it is no wonder that the image became institutionalized. It kept alive the myth that blacks were "inferior" and led to collective putdown labels for blacks, such as "darkies," "coons," "pickaninnies," and "niggers." Although the Sambo image was ripped apart during the civil rights movement of the 1960s, it appears in some forms even today. As one black man explained, "I still see black-faced iron jockeys standing in white folks' lawns making a mockery of black men. And worse, I've had people call me 'Sunshine' or 'Sambo.' I know I have a jovial personality but I'm no fool. People in my town know me well. They can call me by my *name*."

Another negative image that has had a long life in American culture is the Jewish caricature. Almost as commonplace as the Sambo image, it appeared primarily in cartoons, as a stage character, and in anti-Semitic jokes. The caricature constantly portrayed Jews as aggressive, greedy, money-grabbing people. Cartoon figures—male or female—were always shown with prominent noses, and the men were made to appear sly or scheming. The images reflected the WASP hatred for Jews, whom they believed were evil and responsible for the death of Christ.

In addition, the majority of Americans resented Jewish immigrants who managed to rise from rags to riches. Usually the rewards were the result of menial labor, pushcart sales, and careful money management, but these traits were called "pushiness" or "greed." Yet when other groups acquired wealth through the same traits exhibited by Jewish immigrants, the traits were seen as "hard work" and "thrift"—that is, as positive attributes.

In recent years, negative images of Arabs have permeated the American culture. Cartoons, comic strips, illustrations in children's books, and even Halloween costumes have presented Arabs in an unfavorable manner. For example, such comic strips as "Annie," "Brenda Starr," "Broom Hilda," and "The Wizard of Id" have often portrayed Arabs with huge noses and other ugly features and have characterized Arabs as "arrogant, rich oil sheiks," "shifty, menacing villains," or "crooked and greedy." TV wrestlers with names like Akbar the Great and Abdullah the Butcher say they are from the Middle East (but are Americans) and give the impression that they are murderous villains.

The negative images stem from conflicts in the Middle East and the fact that the majority of Americans tend to see all Arabs as terrorists or as responsible for conflicts over the much-needed resource oil. Myths also abound that all Arabs are extremely wealthy and are buying up all the land and businesses in the United States. *None* of these images represents the true characteristics of Arabic-speaking people. Unfortunately, the myths are difficult to combat because most Americans have little understanding of the cultures of Arabic-speaking nations and few look for opportunities to learn.

Putdowns of Native Americans have persisted ever since the first European explorer set foot on the American continent. In written accounts and in visuals, Indians have been presented as "warlike," "uncivilized," "alcoholics," "lazy," and "always living off the government." The stereotypes ignore the fact that a basic value of Indian societies is living in peace with nature. In addition, the federal governments of both the United States and Canada historically have been responsible for the loss of Indian lands, placing Indians on reservations and isolating them from the rest of society, and forcing dependency.

Justifying or making excuses for prejudice by blaming the victim is one more way that racism and bigotry are sustained. Certain traits such as dependency, laziness, greed, and low intelligence are said to be "inborn." In other words, the majority group revives the old idea that people inherit "inferior" and "superior" traits.

As an example, when unemployed people remain jobless, it is easy for those who are employed and financially stable to point their fingers and suggest that the jobless are "just born lazy," "don't want to do for themselves," or "aren't smart enough to find work." The assumption is that the unemployed have brought the problem on themselves. However, unemployment often comes about because factories and businesses close. People cannot afford to move to areas where jobs are available or they need to learn new skills to be placed in jobs.

Economic and political considerations are major factors in continued racism, bigotry, and prejudice. As some sociologists have put it in recent years, racism persists in order to maintain the status quo, or the social structure that now exists. In the United States, members of the white male majority hold most of the political power and also control most of the large corporations and businesses. It is not likely that people within that power structure will *voluntarily* give up their advantages and privileged positions. As a result, when others—minorities or women—try to gain power through economic influence or political office, they are seen as threats. Some members of the power structure then try to combat that threat by denying "outsiders" opportunities for advancement.

However, people within a power structure do not always act in hostile or openly bigoted ways. Rather, there is less obvious prejudice at work, particularly in the business world. Many corporate executives, who are primarily white, conduct business in private clubs or other settings from which blacks, Jews, Arabs, Hispanics, and members of other groups, including women, may be excluded. Minority businesspersons then have few opportunities to develop a supporting network of people who can help pave the way for profitable business deals.

Those outside the power structure also must fight the attitude of corporate managers who believe that businesses run by minorities, particularly blacks, Hispanics, and Native Americans, are not competent. Since most minority companies are service industries or small firms that supply materials for large manufacturers, they depend on corporations for business. Although minority companies receive an increasing amount of business from predominantly white corporations, they seldom can grow and expand as white businesses do.

A case in point was made by a black businessman who opened a travel consulting firm serving corporate executives in New York. Although his business is doing well, the black businessman believes he would be much farther ahead if he were white. To test his theory, the businessman sent out company brochures picturing minorities, and corporations responded with rejection form letters. However, when he sent brochures picturing whites, he received invitations to bid for business.

Black auto dealers have described similar experiences. Many do not publicize their race so that white customers who do not want to deal with blacks will continue to buy from the dealership. Black buyers are also turned off by blacks in business, claims Horace Noble, a black businessman in Chicago who owns two auto dealerships. Noble told a *Chicago Tribune* reporter that black city residents do not like to shop at his city dealership but will go to his suburban dealership because it appears to be a "nice, white" business.

Noble contends that black buyers have accepted the stereotypical notion that black businesspeople are less reliable and honest than whites. To bring in more black customers for his city dealership, Noble plans to hire more white workers and change the business name. "If I make it [the dealership] look white, it will do twice as good," he told the *Tribune* reporter.

In other instances of racism in business, a member of a minority group might apply for an advanced position on a job, but that application easily can be ignored if hiring personnel do not want to allow minorities to move up. Or those who do the hiring may never think of choosing a minority person for a top job. As people of color are kept in low-status positions, the members of the majority can feel justified in saying, "See I told you so! 'Those people' just aren't bright enough (or ambitious enough) to make it!" Thus, the pattern of "inferior" and "superior" groups is maintained.

A prime example of how institutionalized racism is maintained was an incident in January 1988 involving Jimmy "The Greek" Snyder, a CBS sports commentator known for predicting the outcome of sporting events. In a TV interview on *NFL Today*, Snyder rambled on about how blacks have been "bred" for athletics, reinforcing a stereotype that black males are "born athletes" (or physical workers) and thus leaving the impression that blacks are not capable of intellectual achievement. As protests poured into the TV station, CBS dismissed Snyder, saying that the commentator's remarks "in no way reflect the views of CBS Sports."

The Snyder incident came just months after similar stereotypical remarks from Al Champanis were aired during Ted Koppel's *Nightline* show on ABC-TV. Champanis, then a baseball manager, said in a midsummer 1987 interview with Koppel that blacks may lack "some of the necessities" to be managers of sports teams. As *U.S. News & World Report* noted, Champanis's comments revealed "what no whites wanted to believe: Racial stereotypes persist in American sports, barring all but a few blacks from front-office jobs and 'thinking' positions."

One of the few blacks to make it as an executive in professional sports is Bill White, who in 1989 became the first black man to head a national professional sports league. A former All-Star first baseman, White's role as president of the National League may help break down barriers for blacks seeking management positions in other sports. But as far as White is concerned, "You just do the job whether you're red, yellow, purple or whatever," he told reporters.

Still, there are many people of color who face barriers to top jobs because of stereotypes that are based on the old concepts about intelligence—the idea that genes determine the mental abilities of various groups or races. For example, during the period when there was a huge influx of immigrants to the United States, federal officials using interpreters gave IQ (intelligence) tests to the newcomers. Test results showed that the immigrants—Italians, Hungarians, Russians, and Jews from various nations—scored much lower than established Americans of northern European ancestry. This was not surprising given the fact that few immigrants knew the English language. Because of the test results, southern and eastern Europeans were found to be "feeble-minded" and said to be "innately inferior." The test results were hailed as "proof" that some groups of people are "born dumb."

The idea that groups inherit low intelligence has been used in recent history primarily against blacks. During World War I, for example, blacks scored lower than whites on army tests. Using the scores as a basis, Princeton psychologist Carl Brigham wrote a book-length study that concluded "the army tests indicate clearly the intellectual superiority of the Nordic [white] race group." Other experts questioned such an interpretation of the test scores and found that environment played a greater role in how people performed on tests. Northerners, for example, usually scored higher than southerners, whether black or white.

Over the years, some sociologists, psychologists, and other experts on human behavior discredited the idea that intelligence is fixed by heredity. They pointed to social, economic, and political factors that have an impact on how people perform intellectually and also on many other types of human behavior. Brigham himself later noted that his work on intelligence had been racially biased.

However, the issue was brought up again in 1969 by American psychologist Arthur Jensen and was repeated and reinforced by British psychologist Hans Eysenck. Jensen's theory was presented in a long article published in the *Harvard Educational Review*. Essentially, Jensen claimed that blacks were genetically inferior to whites in terms of mental ability. Thus he concluded that schools and other social institutions would be wasting their time trying to devise programs to help blacks achieve. These ideas created such an uproar that many books and articles followed to refute the racist theory. But Jensen's arguments were widely used by white supremacists to support continued segregation in schools and to deny blacks economic opportunities.

Several years after Jensen's article was published, researchers discovered that the racist theory was based on an earlier British study proved to be fraudulent. The author of the study, Sir Cyril Burt, a British scientist, consistently lied about the number of people he had tested for his research. He also manipulated his material to support his belief that intelligence is determined solely by genes—that it is inherited.

The controversy over the relationship between race and intelligence did not end with the scandal over the British scientist's theory. According to Nancy Stepan, a Yale University historian and author of the *Idea of Race in Science*, "Jensen and Eysenck conceded that Burt was guilty of scientific dishonesty, and that his conclusions . . . were unreliable. But Jensen has continued to maintain that there is a considerable body of evidence from other sources" to support his views.

At the same time, critics of Jensen's theories claim just the opposite. "The pity," as Stepan notes, "is that . . . the debate over race and intelligence has probably served to reinforce rather than erase racial stereotypes."

*By playing on people's fears, hate groups can prompt
bigotry and violence.*

4

How Hate Groups Operate

Stereotypes prevail among those who seem consumed with bigotry and racism. Because of their unreasonable hatred for those different from themselves, some people join groups that harass, intimidate, or commit violence. The terror tactics used by hate groups in the United States have caused great suffering and loss among minority group citizens and immigrants.

The brutality of such hate groups as the Ku Klux Klan (KKK or the Klan) has been widely publicized. The KKK was one of the first terrorist groups in the United States, but contrary to popular belief, it began rather innocently after the Civil War. Six veterans of the Confederacy formed a social club—a secret society—and gave themselves the Greek-sounding name, calling members Ghouls, and their leaders by such titles as Grand Cyclops and Grand Magi (today leaders are known as Grand Dragons or Imperial Wizards).

As a way to amuse themselves without revealing their identities, the new society members disguised themselves in sheets and rode on horseback through their little town of Pulaski, Tennessee. "The ride created such a stir that the men decided to

45

adopt the sheets as the official regalia of the Ku Klux Klan, and they added to the effect by making grotesque masks and tall pointed hats," reported Klanwatch, a project of a civil rights organization called the Southern Poverty Law Center. Klanwatch was set up in 1980 to increase awareness of the KKK's violent nature and to provide legal help for victims of KKK terror tactics.

Membership in the Klan grew, and the night riders began to harass and frighten newly freed blacks. Harassment and intimidation had been common during slavery, when many southern whites, especially plantation owners, feared slave revolts. They believed that blacks would turn against them in revenge for forced labor in cotton and tobacco fields and their years of humiliation and demeaning servitude to "white masters." White southerners also formed mounted patrols to look for, capture, and punish runaway slaves.

After the Civil War, there were still widespread fears that freed slaves would seek revenge or gain political control if allowed to vote and own property. Many poor, white southerners also believed that blacks would take over their jobs. To continue their domination over blacks, some of the southern states adopted Black Codes—laws that said "people of African descent cannot be considered as citizens of the United States."

The Black Codes, in effect, once again made slaves of black people by denying them property and voting rights and by restricting them to menial jobs. To further exercise white domination over blacks, night riders—primarily Klan members—began to ride into black settlements attempting to frighten blacks into submission.

Although verbal threats from white-robed riders could certainly intimidate many people, some blacks were not easily frightened. So the Klan turned to more violent tactics, whipping, mutilating, shooting, and lynching innocent black people.

46

KKK terrorism to instill fear in black communities continued unabated until the end of the 1860s, when federal laws were passed to outlaw Klan activities.

The organization seemed to disband, but the Klan did not disappear. After the turn of the century, the Klan was revived, died out, and was revived again a number of times, with leaders loudly proclaiming their views on white—WASP—supremacy. The KKK attacked not only blacks but also Jews, Catholics, immigrants, and women who fought for voting and other civil rights and job opportunities.

The Klan claims to be Christian and to hold patriotic American views. But the organization has consistently carried out activities that show disdain for Christian beliefs and for democratic principles, both of which respect the dignity and worth of people from all different backgrounds.

Over the years many Klansmen have been consumed with hate for people who are different from themselves. Male and female victims of Klan brutality have been tarred and feathered and have suffered floggings, torture, and death. In some instances the Klan branded those they considered "un-American" with acid, burning the initials KKK on victims' foreheads. Attacks against and murder of fellow humans frequently went on with the silent support of law officials and many community leaders, who turned their backs in secret approval of the Klan violence.

After World War II, American society began to change somewhat as soldiers came home. Many black, Asian, Hispanic and other minority veterans had fought for world freedom but were being denied freedom at home. Across the United States, groups organized to protest acts of discrimination and violence against minorities. At the same time, Congress passed a number of federal civil rights laws, and many civic leaders and law officials no longer tolerated the crimes of Klan members.

Nevertheless, the Klan's campaign for white supremacy continued. From the mid-1950s through the 1960s, a time when many thousands of civil rights activists were at work, Klan members were responsible for hundreds of violent attacks against minority groups and civil rights workers. According to Klanwatch, "From 1956-1963 alone the Klan was suspected of 138 bombings across the South." During that time, the Klan's terrorist activities also resulted in the burning of black churches, the castration of a black man, and murders of civil rights workers and a black army colonel. The Federal Bureau of Investigation (FBI) and state officials investigated, arrested, and prosecuted Klan members, convicting some KKK leaders and thus preventing some violence.

The number of Klan members nationwide has dropped dramatically in recent years, from about 10,000 in 1981 to about 5,000 today. But Klan attacks and rallies have gone on:

•In 1981, Klansmen harassed Vietnamese fishermen in Galveston Bay, Texas, burning their boats and homes and trying to frighten the recent immigrants so that they would leave the area.

•In 1981, Klansmen in Mobile, Alabama, attacked Michael Donald, a young black man who was walking to the store for a pack of cigarettes. The Klansmen brutally beat and strangled Donald, slit his throat, and hanged him from a tree. Two Klansmen were convicted, and one was sentenced to die for the crime. Then in 1987, the Southern Poverty Law Center (SPLC) and its Klanwatch project supported by other civil rights groups sued the KKK on behalf of the Donald family. The civil suit charged that the KKK was liable for actions of its members. In an unprecedented decision, a federal

48

court agreed and ordered the KKK to pay the Donald family $7 million in damages

•In 1983, Klansmen bombed the Montgomery, Alabama, offices of the Southern Poverty Law Center in an attempt to destroy evidence investigators for the center had gathered showing illegal Klan acts.

•In 1984, a KKK-sponsored cable TV station and electronic "bulletin boards" for computer operators were set up in various parts of the nation to spread hate messages, some of which advocate the killing of Jews and people of color.

•In 1985, a Klan unit was found operating within law enforcement agencies in the Louisville, Kentucky, area.

•In 1986, investigators exposed active-duty U.S. military personnel who were training Klansmen in military tactics and funneling military arms and explosives into the Klan's paramilitary army headquartered in North Carolina.

•In 1987, Klan members jeered, shouted insults, and threw bottles and rocks at peaceful civil rights marchers in Forsyth County, Georgia, causing injuries to several marchers. Not long afterward Klansmen paraded through College Park, Georgia, a suburb of Atlanta, carrying signs with such slogans as "God segregated them, white trash integrated them" and "Thank God for AIDS." The latter slogan refers to the white supremacist belief that AIDS eventually will wipe out people of color as well as homosexuals.

•In 1988, a Connecticut Klan group traveled to Dallas, Texas, to stage a rally in front of the city hall protesting the Dallas police department's new affirmative action hiring plan.

Wherever the Klan demonstrates, members spout their belief in white supremacy, and spokesmen for a "New Klan" frequently spew their hatred and belief in violent, lawless action to achieve their goals. "If you've got in your mind to go out here and break the law . . . just go out and do it. Don't tell anybody . . . . Back in the old days the sheriff was in the Klan. You didn't have to worry about it. I wish them days was back. But they ain't going to come back until we bring them back." Those are the words of Glenn Miller, once head of the White Patriot Party (WPP), a Klan group in North Carolina.

Miller was arrested in 1987 on conspiracy charges. In a legal bargaining arrangement, he agreed to provide names of White Patriot members in exchange for pleading guilty to a lesser charge of sending threatening letters through the U.S. mails. Miller was sentenced to five years in prison and fined $250,000.

A number of Klan groups such as WPP have close ties with neo-Nazis—groups who try to keep Hitler's ideas alive. Recent reports indicate that neo-Nazis in the United States are linked with a network of neo-Nazis in Europe who have been active since the end of World War II. The European network of neo-Nazis is reportedly responsible for terrorist activities against American citizens and U.S. Army installations in Europe.

Like their European counterparts, neo-Nazis in the United States usually read books about Nazi beliefs, watch video tapes on Hitler, sometimes tattoo themselves with swastikas, wear military garb, and practice guerrilla and terrorist maneuvers. Neo-Nazis also accept as gospel the views of such white supremacists as Canadian Ernst Zundel, who has written hate literature against Jews. Zundel falsely claimed that the Holocaust did not happen. The Canadian government successfully prosecuted Zundel for willfully promoting hatred and sentenced him to fifteen months in prison.

In recent years, neo-Nazis have recruited gangs of youths who shave their heads and call themselves skinheads or "skins." A special report from the Anti-Defamation League of B'nai B'rith (ADL), a civil rights and human relations group, noted in late 1987, "The number of skinhead activists at present is small—no more than several hundred across the country—but they are growing." Skinheads glorify violence and are closely associated with hard rock "white power" music, which includes such songs as "Nigger, Nigger" and a ballad that glorifies Rudolf Hess. Hess was a notorious Nazi war criminal who was sentenced to life imprisonment in 1946 and died in Spandau Prison in West Berlin, Germany, in 1987.

Skinhead groups first organized in Britain during the 1970s. They dressed and acted like street toughs and spouted anti-immigrant slogans. British neo-Nazis enrolled a number of skinheads who reportedly have been involved in riots, street battles, and other violence.

In the United States, skinheads also have been linked with violence. Members of skinhead groups have been arrested for crimes ranging from assault to robbery in such cities as Chicago, Cincinnati, Detroit, Los Angeles, and San Francisco.

Not all young people attracted to skinhead groups and white power music are neo-Nazis, and hard-core membership in neo-Nazi groups "has declined steadily . . . from a peak of 1,000-1,200 in 1978 to no more than 400-450 in 1987, the ADL report noted. But ADL officials fear the "present rise of the skinhead gangs could bring about a reversal of that downward trend."

Some U.S. neo-Nazi members are also aligned with the Identity Church, a religious cult whose leaders preach that Jews are descendants of Satan and mated with animals, producing "mud races," or nonwhite people. One Identity leader, Robert Miles, is a former convict who blew up six school buses in Pontiac, Michigan, when the city's public schools desegregated. Miles, who calls himself a pastor of the Mountain Church of Jesus Christ the Savior, has recruited ex-convicts for his church in Cohoctah, Michigan. Miles wrote in a newsletter (in capital letters), "WE BELIEVE THAT WE WERE CREATED IN THE ASTRAL KINGDOM BY OUR GOD, WHO WAS THE FIRST WHITE EVER. WE BELIEVE THAT WE WERE SENT TO THIS EARTH TO SUBDUE IT AND TO QUELL THE REBELLION RAGING UNDER THE LEADERSHIP OF SATANEL, THE REX MUNDI. UNTIL WE COMPLETE THAT TASK, WE SHALL FIND NO PEACE NOR REST. WE ARE THE SOLDIERS OF THE KING WHO IS OUR GOD AND OUR ONLY GOVERNMENT. OUR ASTRAL RACE IS OUR ONLY NATION."

During a 1987 Halloween celebration, which Miles in his writings calls Samhain and declares "is only the White Race's holiday," the preacher called on the "folk to stand as fast and firm in their faith as Rudolf Hess." Miles told his followers that Hess was "one of the true heroes of our race" and urged the group "to reclaim the heritage and honor of being German-Americans." For help, Miles suggested contacting the German-American Information and Education Association (GAIEA), which is under the direction of a Hans Schmidt.

Officials of ADL say that Schmidt served in the Waffen SS, a unit of Hitler's army that operated concentration camps and massacred civilians. Another GAIEA leader is Stan Rittenhouse, who has been an aide for a Washington, D.C., lobbying group that works for neo-Nazi and KKK causes.

Not only did Miles praise Hess. Miles also condemned the American government, which he and other Identity preachers falsely say is Jewish-controlled. Miles called the federal government "the worst enemy of the white race." He told the group of a few hundred followers that he would defy the "devil federals" who had "lied" and charged him with sedition, or conspiring to overthrow the U.S. government. But Miles in his own words declares that the U.S. government should be replaced with a "theocratic republic" (ruled by God) for whites only. The racist goal would be achieved through military action—terrorism and violence, by increasing families in the white supremacist movement, and by passing a U.S. constitutional amendment that would deny citizenship to all minorities in the United States.

Another who shares Miles's views is Richard G. Butler, a self-proclaimed minister who heads a neo-Nazi Identity group known as Aryan Nations. Headquarters for the Aryan Nations is a fenced compound near Hayden, Idaho. During the early 1970s, members of the Aryan Nations—neo-Nazis, Klansmen, Identity Church followers—began working to establish a whites-only homeland in the northwestern states of Idaho, Montana, Wyoming, Oregon, and Washington.

At first, most residents of northern Idaho ignored the Aryan Nations who were handing out racist handbills and preaching their bigoted views. The Aryan Nations appeared to be eccentric or absurd, a lunatic fringe group. But beginning in the 1980s, racist and anti-Jewish activities increased in northern Idaho. A neo-Nazi, now in jail, distributed an ugly poster called an "Official Runnin' Nigger Target" to be used for shooting practice. Along with the poster came "The Aryan Nation District of Idaho Nigger Hunting License" which supposedly gave the racist holder the license to "hunt and kill niggers during the open season."

Swastikas—Nazi symbols—were painted on churches and public buildings in Coeur d'Alene, a city on the Idaho-Washington border. A family with adopted minority children received hate mail and threats. The home of a Catholic priest, a civil rights activist, was bombed, and several bombs exploded in the federal building at Coeur d'Alene.

In 1984, Alan Berg, a well-known and outspoken radio talk show host and a Jew, was gunned down outside his Denver, Colorado, home. Evidence linked the murder to one time

53

members of the Aryan Nations who had followed the teachings of Richard Butler. The murderers were part of a terror group called The Order, which had split from the Aryan Nations. By the end of 1984, federal agents had arrested twenty three members of The Order. Some turned informants and pleaded guilty, drawing twenty year prison terms. Others were charged with armed robbery, murder, counterfeiting, and plotting the overthrow of the U.S. government.

Since the early 1980s, the racist activities of the Aryan Nations in the Northwest have been monitored by a citizen action group in Idaho known as the Kootenai County Task Force on Human Relations. A Task Force leader, Norman Gissel, who is an attorney in Coeur d'Alene, pointed out that the Task Force is a "grassroots" organization and that members have been able "to mobilize public opinion," drawing support "from politicians of all persuasions, both liberal and conservative, from ordinary citizens, and from the more traditional service groups such as Kiwanis, Lions, and Rotary, as well as from the mainstream religious groups." As a result of Task Force efforts, the Idaho legislature passed one of the toughest laws in the nation prohibiting malicious harassment. The law specifically states:

> It shall be unlawful for any person, maliciously and with the specific intent to intimidate or harass another person because of the person's race, color, religion, ancestry, or national origin, to:
>
> (a) Cause physical injury to another person; or
>
> (b) Damage, destroy, or deface any real or personal property of another person; or
>
> (c) Threaten, by word or act, to do the acts prohibited if there is reasonable cause to believe that any of the acts described in subsections (a) and (b) of this section will occur.
>
> For purposes of this section, "deface" shall include, but not be limited to, cross-burnings or the placing of any word or symbol commonly associated with racial, religious or ethnic

terrorism on the property of another person without his or her permission.

The criminal penalty for breaking the law is imprisonment for up to five years or a fine of up to $5,000 or both. Because of the state law, officials have been able to arrest and convict offenders and significantly cut down the number of harassment cases.

In addition to supporting the state legislation, the Kootenai County Task Force helped establish a Northwest Coalition Against Malicious Harassment with over 140 members representing various civic and religious groups and government agencies from a five-state area and parts of Canada. The Task Force also has sponsored human rights and "Good Neighbor" celebrations. One purpose of the celebrations was expressed in 1986 by John V. Evans, then Governor of Idaho, in a speech for a Good Neighbor Day in Coeur d'Alene:

> We want everyone to know that the Aryan Nations and other such hate groups do *not* represent nor do they speak for the people of Idaho. Although small in number, these hate groups have a blind and unreasoning intolerance for diversity . . . . Victims . . . are primarily ethic and religious minorities. But we are all in danger of becoming victims if we allow intimidation and fear to prevail.
>
> It is important for all of us to remember that the strength of our democratic nation . . . derives from the diversity of our people.

Similar views were expressed at the first national conference on "Prejudice and Violence in America" held in September 1986 in Crystal City, Virginia, just outside Washington, D.C. Sponsored by a nonprofit private research group called the National Institute Against Prejudice and Violence, the conference "grew out of the Institute's conviction

55

that violence and intimidation motivated by racial, religious, or ethnic bigotry is a serious, pervasive problem in the United States which has not received adequate attention." During the two-day event, participants discussed "ethnoviolence"—violence against ethnic groups, or people defined by their racial, religious, or national backgrounds—and what might be done to prevent it. The conference drew representatives from criminal justice, law enforcement, human and civil rights agencies, education, and the media.

One of the major speakers was the director of the FBI, William Webster, who pointed out that federal laws allow his department to legally investigate groups or individuals who violate others' civil rights or the U.S. Constitution or who use "force and violence for political ends." Webster explained that the FBI keeps close track of not only the Aryan Nations and the Klan but such groups as the "Covenant, the Sword and the Arm of the Lord, a paramilitary survivalist group headquartered in Arkansas who believes in the racial inferiority of Jews, blacks and Orientals . . . [and] has close ties with both the Aryan Nations and the Order."

Other hate groups under FBI surveillance include the Sheriff's Posse Comitatus, which has no central nationwide organization but is actively anti-Jewish and anti-black, and such white supremacist groups as the Christian Patriots Defense League, Illium City, the National Alliance, and White Americans Resistance. Webster noted that the FBI also follows the activities of "racially violent groups that target whites . . . . One is the New African Freedom Fighters, a militant left-wing group that was started by Latula Chakoor, a recently arrested top-ten fugitive . . . . We are probing Jewish extremist elements that have claimed responsibility for murders of Arab targets in our country, such as Alexander Codas in Los Angeles, who was the head of the American Arab Anti-Discrimination Committee whose office was bombed causing his death."

Webster pointed out, as did other conference participants, that most hate groups operate in secret and though small in number are "proficient in paramilitary training. Many are trained through military experience. They are highly skilled, both with weapons and with explosives. To combat these groups, a close working relationship between law enforcement and the public is absolutely essential," Webster said.

Another danger posed by hate groups is possible "copycat" behavior. The rhetoric and violence of hate groups can stimulate others to act out their prejudices. Hate groups also try to stir up the public by scapegoating, blaming racial or ethnic group members for problems that are national in scope, such as farms lost to bankruptcies, the loss of manufacturing jobs to other nations, or increasing crime rates. By playing on people's fears and dissatisfactions, hate groups can prompt even more acts of ethnoviolence.

Martin Luther King, Jr.'s message of nonviolent protest inspired many in the struggle for civil rights.

5

The Struggle for Civil Rights

Violence marched side by side with nonviolence during the late 1950s and through the 1960s in the United States. During this historic period, the struggle against racism and for the civil rights of people of color frequently meant putting one's life on the line.

Hundreds of articles, books, TV shows, and films have documented the many events of the civil rights movement, which some historians have called a revolution. It was a revolution in the sense that people set out to peacefully change a way of life, particularly in southern states where segregation laws established separate facilities such as restrooms and fountains for "White" and "Colored." Apartments and hotels carried signs to indicate "White Only" or "Colored Only." Restaurants, laundromats, and movie theaters owned or operated by whites refused to serve people of color.

Discrimination against people because of their skin color was not confined to the South, however. Across the nation blacks and other minorities were barred from certain jobs and professions, were not allowed to rent or buy homes in certain neighborhoods, and usually attended separate schools with far fewer facilities and resources than all-white schools.

Before the 1950s, a few changes came about, such as President Harry Truman's commission to deal with discrimination in government jobs and the banning of dining-car segregation on railroads. With Jackie Robinson leading the way, blacks joined previously all-white major league baseball teams, and some major universities began to admit blacks and other minorities. Still, these were only beginning steps in efforts to overturn discriminatory laws and segregation in the United States.

One of the first major changes in federal laws that helped propel the civil rights movement was the decision in the now well-known case of *Brown* v. *Board of Education of Topeka*. Oliver Brown of Topeka, Kansas, wanted his daughter, Linda, to attend a school just a few blocks from where the family lived. But the state had set up segregated schools, which the Supreme Court years before had decided was constitutional according to a federal law that required "separate but equal" facilities.

The educational facilities for blacks and whites were not equal, however, as investigators—both black and white—had often pointed out. That fact and Mr. Brown's belief that his daughter should be able to attend a neighborhood school rather than have to ride in a rickety bus to a black school miles away prompted action. When the school board refused to let Linda attend the nearby school, Mr. Brown, with the help of the National Association for the Advancement of Colored People (NAACP), took the case to the Supreme Court.

In May 1954, the Court overturned the earlier federal "separate but equal" law and ordered that public schools be desegregated "with all deliberate speed." The Supreme Court ruling led to desegregation of some public schools, but not without mob protests and outright defiance of the federal law. Later Supreme Court rulings banned segregation in interstate travel and segregation on public buses. Then in 1957, Congress passed a Civil Rights Bill, the first since 1875, which was designed to set up a civil rights division in the Justice Department and to protect black voting rights and the right of blacks to sit on a jury.

Putting federal laws in place was only one part of the struggle for black freedom and opportunity, as a recent TV series, *Eyes on the Prize*, and a companion book with the same title clearly show. In a preface to the printed version of *Eyes on the Prize*, Henry Hampton, the executive producer and creator of the TV series, explained why he put together the documentary, which chronicles the period from 1954 to 1965. Hampton wrote that he wanted to fulfill a dream to "capture the magnificent spirit of the Americans" who struggled for racial equality . . . [and] to preserve this piece of American history so that it might be taught to tomorrow's children as well."

The series and the book written by Juan Williams are filled with stories about real people—ordinary people as well as leaders and movers—who had the courage and fortitude to fight for freedom. Some of the "ordinary people" were also those on the sidelines who became victims, people such as black teenager Emmett Till.

In 1955, Till was only fourteen years old and had a speech defect brought on by polio. He lived in Chicago but was visiting relatives in Mississippi. Till was dragged from his relatives' home and was brutally beaten; his head was bashed in, an eye gouged out, and he was tossed in the river with a seventy-five-pound fan tied with barbed wire around his neck. What had brought on such brutality? Supposedly he had flirted with a young white woman. His murderers, who sat in court smugly smoking cigars and denying the ugly deed, were found "not guilty" by an all-white jury who had been warned by the judge not to convict the killers.

Many Americans were shocked and incensed at the barbarity of killing an innocent child to maintain white supremacy. Till's death mobilized many blacks and whites to work for equal protection under the law and against segregation and discrimination.

One of the major civil rights efforts was to overturn laws that segregated public buses in the South. Black people were forced to ride in the back of public buses and had to stand even when there were empty seats. When Rosa Parks, a black woman who had been working all day, refused to give up her seat to a white person on a Montgomery, Alabama, bus, she broke one of the state's segregation laws. She was arrested and jailed. The NAACP took Parks's case to the Supreme Court. As blacks learned about the case, they began to organize a boycott of the city's bus system, which lasted more than a year. The boycott financially hurt the bus company and downtown businesses that catered to bus riders, who were mostly black.

Although the Supreme Court ruled that segregation on public buses was illegal, the nonviolent boycott brought violence against blacks. Some whites retaliated by arresting black leaders, bombing black homes, and shooting and beating black people. Still, nonviolent demonstrations went on as citizens pressed for desegregation in public facilities of all kinds in the South.

To help call attention to segregation in Birmingham, Alabama, the Southern Christian Leadership Conference (SCLC), a group of ministers working for social justice, asked Martin Luther King, Jr., to help stage a huge demonstration in the spring of 1963. The plan was to conduct a massive, nonviolent march. In addition, the SCLC planned a boycott of downtown businesses.

When the march took place, police used water hoses, dogs,

and cattle prods against the marchers and, as expected, arrested King along with many others. While King was in the Birmingham jail, a group of white clergymen publicly deplored King's part in the demonstration. In an open letter published in the local newspaper, the clergy said that the black leader should wait for a better time to stage massive marches.

King wrote a reply from his Birmingham jail cell, eloquently pointing out how "This 'Wait' has almost always meant 'Never.'" King's letter was first printed and distributed by Quakers, members of a religious group that preaches nonviolence, and then it was reprinted in many national publications. An excerpt from that letter follows:

> Perhaps it is easy for those who have never felt the stinging darts of segregation to say "Wait." But when you have seen vicious mobs lynch your mothers and fathers at will and drown your sisters and brothers at whim, when you have seen hate-filled policemen curse, kick, and even kill your black brothers and sisters; when you see the vast majority of your twenty million Negro brothers smothering in an airtight cage of poverty in the midst of an affluent society; when you suddenly find your tongue twisted and your speech stammering as you seek to explain to your six-year-old daughter why she can't go to the public amusement park that has just been advertised on television, and see tears welling up in her eyes when she is told that Funtown is closed to colored children, and see ominous clouds of inferiority beginning to form in her little mental sky, and see her beginning to distort her personality by developing an unconscious bitterness toward white people; when you have to concoct an answer for a five-year-old son who is asking, "Daddy, why do white people treat colored people so mean?" .... then you will understand why we find it difficult to wait.

King's efforts as well as those of many other activists helped bring about major gains in civil rights. Blacks and whites, men and women, and people from varied religious backgrounds and from northern and southern states took part in "freedom marches" and public demonstrations in the South to demand racial equality.

One mass demonstration for civil rights was held in August 1963 at the Lincoln Memorial in Washington, D.C. More than 250,000 demonstrators from across the nation joined to let members of Congress know that a strong federal Civil Rights Act was needed to end racial discrimination. King was one of the speakers that day. Again, his words were carried across the land, this time via TV broadcasts and also newspapers and magazines. In his now-famous "I Have a Dream" speech, King described his dream for racial equality and the day "when all God's children, black men and white men, Jews and gentiles, Protestants and Catholics, will be able to join hands and sing in the words of the old Negro spiritual: 'Free at last. Free at last. Thank God Almighty, we are free at last.'"

Freedom would not come easily, however. Many civil rights workers—both black and white—were in constant danger. Some were shot and wounded. Others were killed.

During this turbulent period, the president of the United States, John F. Kennedy, was assassinated. His successor, President Lyndon Johnson, helped convince Congress to pass strong federal civil rights legislation. One of the laws, the Voting Rights Act of 1965, banned the qualifying tests blacks were required to pass in some southern communities before they could register to vote. But the federal law was not enforced easily. Mobs of whites carrying guns, knives, and clubs frequently prevented blacks from voting.

Continued brutality and discrimination led to riots in some cities during the 1960s and to a militant Black Power movement. Black Power meant different things to different people, however. To the leaders of the NAACP in the mid-1960s, Black Power was "the father of hatred and the mother of violence." To leaders of the Congress of Racial Equality (CORE), founded more than twenty years earlier by University

64

of Chicago students, Black Power emphasized "pride, self-respect and participation and control of one's destiny and community affairs." To militant leaders such as Stokely Carmichael, the idea of Black Power was to show that blacks needed to unite in strength, to be proud of their culture and willing to fight for justice.

Blacks were not the only minority group struggling for civil rights during the 1960s. Mexican Americans and Native Americans, for example, faced discrimination and began to organize so that their rights would also be recognized. Mexican Americans, who called themselves Chicanos, organized a national union to gain higher wages for farm laborers, many of whom were Mexican Americans. On Indian reservations, Native Americans took steps to gain control over their own affairs, taking charge of police, education, and social programs that had been run by federal agents.

Women also joined the civil rights movement. Although not a minority in number, women faced minority status in jobs, education, and political power. Women's groups helped establish the federal law that prohibits job discrimination not only on the basis of race but also on the basis of gender. In addition, demands for equality helped women win elections to Congress and to state and local offices. Women also have taken leadership positions in other areas of society. In February 1989, for example, Barbara Harris, a black, became the first woman to be consecrated an Episcopal Church bishop.

Other changes that can be traced to the civil rights movement include federal and state laws that prohibit segregation in public schools and discrimination in housing. Today, more and more people of minority status as well as the handicapped are able to acquire better jobs and to protect their civil rights. But in spite of great advances over a thiry-year period, members of some ethnic and racial groups still struggle for equal opportunities and for justice.

*At one time, it was believed that women did not have the
capabilities required to be educated or to vote.*

6

Equal Justice and Opportunities?

Loyal Garner, Jr., was known as "one of the most respected and liked citizens of Florien, Louisiana," and had never been in trouble with the law. But on Christmas Day 1987 he was arrested by three lawmen in the nearby town of Hemphill, Texas. Garner, a thirty-four-year-old black man, had been on his way with two friends to pick up a car that had become disabled just across the Texas border.

Two county deputies jailed the three black men, throwing them in the drunk tank. When Mr. Garner asked to exercise his right to call his wife, who expected him to be gone only a few hours, the lawmen made it clear that they would not allow the call. Garner began to protest. According to the sworn testimony of one of Mr. Garner's friends, Police Chief Thomas Ladner entered the cell and began to beat Garner with a "slap jack," a piece of lead covered with leather. As Garner continued to protest, he was pulled from the cell and taken to another part of the jail. His friends could hear his moans and cries and the sound of the slap jack for the next half hour.

When Garner was thrown back into the cell, his shirt was soaked with blood and he was breathing heavily. He spent the night on the floor, not moving, his eyes wide open. The next morning he was taken unconscious to the hospital, where Mrs. Garner saw her husband and described him as "unrecognizable." Loyal Garner, Jr., was pronounced dead on December 27, 1987. Along with his widow, Mrs. Corinne Garner, six young children survive him.

On January 4, 1988, the Hemphill police chief and two sheriff's deputies, "Bo" Hyden and Bill Horton of Sabine County, Texas, were indicted by a grand jury for violating Mr. Garner's civil rights, a charge which law officials said was more appropriate than a homicide indictment. Three weeks later a grand jury in the county where Mr. Garner died indicted the lawmen for murder after a coroner's inquest ruled that Garner's death was a homicide. But a Texas Court ruled in mid-August 1988 that trying the men for murder would constitute double jeopardy, or two trials for the same crime. The ruling is being appealed.

Although brutality against blacks and other people of color in the United States is not as widespread as it once was, there are still many cases on record of blacks being falsely accused and wrongly imprisoned. According to studies, blacks seem to suffer more than members of other groups from such civil rights violations. One case was dramatized in a made-for-TV movie, *Guilty of Innocence: The Lenell Geter Story*, shown on CBS in early 1987.

Geter, a black engineer who lives in Greenville, Texas, was arrested in 1982 as a suspect in an armed robbery of a fast-food restaurant. The all-white Dallas County jury convicted Geter of the crime and also heard testimony that suggested he was involved in other fast-food robberies. Geter maintained he was innocent but was sentenced to life imprisonment.

68

A 1983 CBS *60 Minutes* report on the case pointed up that some of Geter's coworkers had seen Geter far from the fast-food restaurant at the time the crime had taken place, but the coworkers had not been asked to testify. The *Dallas Times Herald* previously had carried articles that cast doubt on the trial evidence. A few weeks later, Dallas Country District Attorney Henry Wade joined defense attorneys in asking for a new trial for Geter. In March 1984 after all charges against Geter were dismissed, he was freed. Police had found a new suspect, who was eventually convicted of the armed robberies.

In 1987 Geter filed a civil suit against the prosecutors and police who had wrongfully sent him to prison. The miscarriage of justice, as Geter's lawyer described it, "could happen anywhere."

A similar search for justice is underway for another black man, Clarence Lee Brandley, who has been sentenced to die. A former janitor in a Texas high school, he was convicted of the rape and murder of a sixteen-year-old girl. Twice his execution has been stayed because witnesses have changed their stories, accusing another man. Some evidence in the case also was lost.

In early 1987, James McCloskey, a Philadelphia businessman who founded the Centurian Ministries to aid people believed to be wrongly imprisoned, began to investigate the Brandley case. McCloskey, who asks no fee for his work, was involved in a widely publicized effort to release another black man, Nate Walker of New Jersey. Walker spent eight years in prison for a rape he did not commit. He was freed in November 1986 after McCloskey found evidence, previously overlooked, that proved Walker could not have been the rapist.

Along with a struggle for equal justice, many members of minorities also face glaring inequities in job opportunities. The

Civil Rights Act of 1964 attempted to deal with inequities in jobs and income by outlawing segregation and discrimination, but those who hold economic power do not give it up easily. A number of studies over the past twenty to twenty-five years have revealed a wide gap between the incomes of whites and those of non-whites, who are often relegated to low-paying jobs such as household workers, cooks, welfare aides, baggage porters, farm laborers, and elevator operators. White males dominate higher-paying jobs and hold most of the supervisory positions. As a result, poverty levels are far higher among blacks, Hispanics, and Native Americans than among whites.

Another part of the 1960s legislation was an executive order signed by President Johnson that called for affirmative action. That is, firms doing business with the federal government must make good-faith efforts to hire and promote members of minority groups for jobs from which minorities previously have been excluded. Also, universities receiving federal funds are required to recruit minority students.

Affirmative action was intended to address wrongs of the past, to equalize educational and hiring opportunities for minority groups. As an example, affirmative action had a part in increasing the number of black police officers in the nation from about 24,000 in 1970 to over 43,000 in 1980. Before the advent of civil rights legislation, blacks and other people of color were seldom considered, let alone hired, for jobs that carried any kind of authority. Along with federal financial aid programs, affirmative action also helped bring more minority students into universities and colleges than ever before.

However, a commission that included former presidents Gerald Ford and Jimmy Carter plus other political, educational, and civic leaders released a report in May 1988 showing that efforts to achieve equality for minority groups had slowed or in some cases moved backward since the late 1970s. Leaders of the Commission on Minority Participation in Education and American Life noted that there were still wide economic, educational, and social gaps between minorities—black, Hispanic, and Native American groups—and the majority white group. In its report, the commission declared, "In the last ten years, not only have we lost the momentum of earlier minority progress, we have suffered actual reversals in the drive to achieve full equality for minority citizens." The commission did not place blame for inequities but called for "a new vision of affirmative action around which a broad national consensus can be formed."

Yet there have been and still are many critics of affirmative action. In fact, early in Reagan's presidency, he made clear that his administration would try to overturn the executive order that established affirmative action. The administration also set out to remove other federal regulations that Reagan called "intrusions in our lives that have resulted from unnecessary and excessive growth of government." The president's solicitor general, who argues a case on the side supported by the president, on a number of occasions argued in court on behalf of those against affirmative action and other civil rights laws. Examples include the administration's support of a tax exemption for private schools that discriminate against blacks and attempts to weaken enforcement of voting rights laws (which Congress blocked by a wide majority).

According to critics, affirmative action programs allow for racial preference and quotas that benefit one group at the expense of others. Some have called it "reverse discrimination." In fact, in a celebrated 1977 case, a white man, Allan Bakke, applied for admission to the University of California medical school through a special program for "disadvantaged" students. The program had to that point included primarily nonwhites. When Bakke was denied admission through the program, he sued the school, arguing that minority students with lower test scores than his were accepted. The California Supreme Court ruled in favor of Bakke, in effect saying that he had been discriminated against because he was white. When the decision was appealed to the U.S. Supreme Court, it was upheld in 1978 on the grounds that the medical school could not set aside a specific number of enrollment spaces for minorities only.

In other decisions, the U.S. Supreme Court has favored minorities, *if past discrimination has been clearly shown.* For example, in 1979 white steel workers challenged in a court suit that an on-the-job training program setting aside half the positions for blacks was reverse discrimination. The Supreme Court ruled in favor of the program because it was a voluntary effort "to abolish traditional patterns" of discrimination in the steel industry.

Another Court ruling in 1986 said that blacks and Hispanics should be favored for firefighting jobs in Cleveland to compensate for a record of past discrimination. Again, in 1987, the Supreme Court in a 5-4 decision upheld a plan requiring that half the promotions in the Alabama Department of Public Safety (the state police force) go to blacks. Writing for the Court, Justice William Brennan, Jr., noted, "For almost four decades, the Department has excluded blacks from all positions, including jobs in the upper ranks." In the Court's opinion such "discriminatory conduct" justified the "race-conscious relief" ordered by a lower court.

The justices who dissented included Chief Justice William Rehnquist, who has long opposed affirmative action. In 1979, Rehnquist wrote that "there is perhaps no device more destructive to the notion of equality than . . . the quota," which he called "a two-edged sword that must demean one in order to prefer the other."

Others who argue against preferential treatment for minority groups say that a large number of Americans—including some minority members—oppose affirmative action programs. One survey showed that one out of ten white Americans believes that he or she has been affected personally by "reverse discrimination." Most believe that jobs and enrollments in colleges should be based on merit, or a person's qualifications or abilities. But who makes those decisions? What determines "merit"?

In the past, "merit" frequently has been based on social and economic status. For example, only the wealthy were thought to be qualified to attend schools in the United States during the early days of the nation. Merit has also meant that only males (usually only white males) were qualified for top jobs, schooling, and voting privileges. It was commonly believed that young women did not have the abilities necessary to master formal schooling and did not have the capabilities required to vote.

Since the early part of this century, tests have been used to determine a person's abilities, aptitudes, and knowledge. But tests often have built-in biases and may be unintentionally designed to favor the majority groups. For example, one researcher recently found that whites do better than blacks on tests that depend on written materials. But blacks outperform whites on tests that depend on oral information. Other research indicates that women may have lower scores than men on tests that measure aptitude for success in college, but women usually get higher grade scores than men in college courses. There also are questions about what qualifications determine how well a person will do in higher education or on a job.

Another argument against affirmative action programs says that minorities, the handicapped, or women may feel they have less self-worth if they receive preferential treatment. Such an argument has not been proven true, and a case in point is President Reagan's appointment of Sandra Day O'Connor to the Supreme Court. Justice O'Connor was not chosen simply on merit; she had no national recognition as a federal judge. Rather, President Reagan had made a campaign promise to appoint more women to judgeships, and his selection of O'Connor came about because of that campaign promise. Yet Justice O'Connor does not seem to be suffering from poor self-esteem because of the fact that being a woman played a part in her appointment to the Court.

Many who have obtained jobs through affirmative action have expressed satisfaction that the doors of opportunity have not automatically slammed shut in their faces. As a visually impaired man who works for a social service agency in the Midwest put it, "I know I am qualified for the job as intake person, and with the help of a Braille computer I function very well. But the agency was not going to hire me until I threatened to file discrimination charges. I am married to another visually impaired person and we maintain our own home as well as most sighted people. We both are able to earn our livelihoods because of affirmative action laws. Without those laws we might be forced to depend on others for our survival."

Another factor seldom considered by those opposed to affirmative action is the fact that jobs filled by minorities, particularly people of color, hardly make a dent in the overall white domination of the economy and social structure in the nation. The male white majority has long received "preferential treatment" in terms of jobs and social status. It is also common for whites who oppose affirmative action to insist that laws and government programs should be based on "color-blind" decisions. But the fact is that most people are color-conscious—often in a negative way. As Supreme Court Justice Harry Blackmun put it, "To get beyond racism, we must first take account of race."

74

For example, most of the justices, including recent appointees, appeared to have a view different from Blackmun's, particularly in regard to a Richmond, Virginia, affirmative action program. Like many governmental units, Richmond established its program in accordance with a Congressional requirement that a portion of federal public works funds be channeled to minority firms; the city set aside 30 percent of its building funds for that purpose. The Richmond program was based on the premise that a tightly knit group of local white contractors had prevented minorities from receiving city building contracts. Although the plan covered most minority groups, half of Richmond's population is black, thus blacks would have been the main beneficiaries. Historically, less than 1 percent of the city building contracts have gone to black firms.

Nevertheless, in early 1989 the Supreme Court, in a 6-3 ruling, struck down the Richmond plan. Writing for the Court, Justice O'Conner found no specific evidence that the city had discriminated against minorities, a requirement for affirmative action. She noted that instead the city had based its program on general discrimination in the nation's past. O'Conner also claimed there were not enough qualified contractors to justify the proportion of funds allocated for affirmative action, a reasoning long used by those trying to avoid minority hiring.

Many private businesses were pleased with the Court decision as was the ADL of B'nai B'rith, which contends it is a "false concept that each racial group is entitled to its share of public jobs and contracts." But other civil rights groups and a number of black leaders believe the ruling is, as Supreme Court Justice Thurgood Marshall wrote in his dissent, "a deliberate and giant step backward in this court's affimative action jurisprudence." Some other legal experts agreed and said the ruling could, within the next decade, jeopardize many government programs designed to promote economic equity for woman and minorities.

Years later, on the anniversary of the night Nazis in Germany smashed the windows of Jewish businesses and synagogues, similar violence still occurs in the United States.

7

Bigotry and Racism: On the Rise?

Black Man Beaten to Death in Jail.
Minorities Displeased With Slow Progress in
Baseball.
Do Colleges Set Asian Quotas?
How Integrated Is America?
Skinhead Gangs Harass Homeless.
A Chilling Wave of Racism.
Police Meet to Discuss Ethnoviolence.
Minnesota Executive Mails Thousands of Hate
Letters to Interracial Families.
Mexican Americans File Discrimination Charges
Against Texas Education System.

These are just a sampling of recent newspaper and magazine headlines that seem to indicate an increase in discriminatory acts and ethnoviolence. *Is* there an increase of bigotry and racism in the United States?

According to a number of reports, crimes committed by *organized* hate groups may be on the decline due to tougher law enforcement and the imprisonment of white supremacist leaders.

However, *individual* acts of ethnoviolence and harassment have been increasing since the mid-1980s. A report from Klanwatch, for example, noted that violence has increased nationwide against blacks and other people of color who move into all-white neighborhoods. Other reports from the state chapters of ADL have shown similar increases in bigoted or racist acts.

Civil rights commissions, which are charged with handling discrimination cases based on religion, color, sex, handicap, or national origin, also have reported that complaints based on race are more numerous. In the midsection of the country, for example, the Indianapolis Civil Rights Commission reported in May 1988 that since 1982 complaints of racism have increased from 45 percent to 55 percent of all cases. Part of that increase is due to the fact that some employers seem more willing to tolerate racist acts but workers are not willing to accept discrimination and are filing complaints.

One discrimination case handled by the Indianapolis Civil Rights Commission was concerned with the way a black man and a white man were disciplined for harassing a female worker. Both men were transferred to other locations, but the black man was sent to a location to which he had no transportation. When the black man would not make the move, he was fired. In this instance, the Civil Rights Commission found that the employer had applied a double standard and had been discriminatory. When employers are found to illegally discriminate, they are usually required to provide the employees with financial or other compensation.

Determining the extent of discrimination and hate violence is difficult because there is no nationwide system to monitor acts of bigotry and racism. To add to the difficulty, law enforcement agencies usually categorize a crime such as defacing a building as vandalism or malicious mischief. A cross burning might be recorded as "burning without a permit," and attacks on people motivated by racist or bigoted beliefs are categorized as "assaults."

Gary Tobin, Ph.D., director of the Center for Modern Jewish Studies at Brandeis University, has conducted a number of surveys to determine whether people believe anti-Semitism is a problem in the United States today. Dr. Tobin pointed out at a national conference, "Prejudice and Violence in America," that overt or outward discrimination against Jews has for the most part "disappeared in the 1980s compared to the 1940s and 1950s, and Jews find themselves well-placed throughout American society."

However, in a recent Center study of sixty communities, Tobin also found that nearly one out of every four Jews said he or she had experienced anti-Semitism during that year, although few believed that there is a lot of anti-Semitism in their communities or in the United States as a whole. The types of anti-Semitic incidents experienced included negative remarks about Jews, harassment, and some discrimination on the job and in housing.

"Nearly nine out of ten Jews who experienced anti-Semitism in any form . . . even violence . . . failed to report that act anywhere. When asked, 'why not?' they said that they didn't think anybody would do anything about it, it wasn't important enough, or they didn't know who to call," Tobin said.

Because of the underreporting of incidents and the data collected in Center studies, Tobin concludes—with caution—that prejudice against Jews has *not* declined in the United States. Another survey of the Midwest also concluded that anti-Semitism was still strong, particularly among some farmers who believe that their financial problems stem from actions of "international Jewish bankers."

Religious bigotry has also surfaced in the political arena. In Chicago, a black member of Mayor Eugene Sawyer's administration, Steve Cokely, publicly accused Jews of "an international conspiracy for world control." Cokely was fired a week later as public criticism mounted. But relations between Jews and blacks became more tense as a black minister, Rev. B. Herbert Martin, defended Cokely by saying in a taped interview with a *Chicago Tribune* reporter that Cokely's statements had "a ring of truth." Martin, chairman of the Chicago Housing Authority and Mayor Sawyer's choice for head of the city's Commission on Human Relations, added, "there is a growing opinion among younger blacks, grassroots black people, that Jews are running things, that Jews are unfair, unloving."

The comments prompted a *Tribune* editorial that criticized not only Martin and Cokely but also Mayor Sawyer for his week-long delay in firing Cokely. These actions, the editorial said, encouraged "other bigots . . . to dig up the embers of anti-Semitism and try to ignite an ugly new racial war in Chicago . . . . If . . . such sick views are 'growing,' it's up to the people of good will to work hard to root out this vicious cancer of anti-Semitism."

Other ministers have also made news with their bigoted remarks. Rev. Bailey Smith, a Southern Baptist minister, claimed during a political rally that "God does not hear the prayer of a Jew." John H. Buchanan, who is chairman of a civil liberties group called People for the American Way and also a Baptist minister, said he was offended by Smith's remark. "Smith is entitled to believe whatever he wants. But he should be ashamed of himself for carrying on in a way which can only serve to spread religious bigotry," Buchanan said.

In another incident, an evangelical minister, Rev. R. L. Hymers of Los Angeles, asked his followers to pray for the death of politicians or judges who did not agree with evangelical views. Rev. Hymers once hired an airplane to carry a banner urging people to pray for the death of Supreme Court Justice William Brennan. In 1987, he publicly prayed that Justice Harry Blackmun, who was about to undergo surgery, would be removed from the bench in "any way that God sees fit." Rev. Hymers said that his prayers would be answered if Blackmun "dies in time for President Reagan to appoint someone who is capable of the job." Both Brennan and Blackmun have supported Supreme Court decisions that uphold a woman's right to have an abortion, decisions that the evangelist and other ultraconservatives want overturned.

Increasingly, there also has been evidence of intolerance and acts of ethnoviolence against American Arabs. Like other ethnic groups, such as Hispanics and Asians, American Arabs are often perceived as having a single religious and national heritage. But American Arabs are evenly divided between the Christian and Muslim faiths and have come from more than twenty Arab nations. The largest number of American Arabs— over 150,000—live in the Detroit area, where many violent incidents have occurred.

In a July 1987 special report for the *Detroit Free Press*, reporter Tom Hundley dramatically outlined problems that American Arab families have faced. Hundley began with the story of Sam and Hanan Warah, who moved into a new home in the suburban community of Westland:

> Neighbors did not take kindly to the Arab American couple. They repeatedly smashed the Warahs' windows; they smeared eggs and human feces on their house and car, and scrawled anti-Arab slogans on the sidewalk.
>
> Once, when the Warahs were away from home, someone broke in, doused several rooms with lighter fluid and lit a match. The fire caused $28,000 in damage.
>
> At the Westland Police Department, there is a thick stack of records documenting all that happened to the Warahs . . . .
>
> In April 1986, on the day U.S. warplanes bombed Libya,

someone sideswiped the family's Cadillac while it was parked in front of their house. A few days later, their mailbox was run over, their child's tricycle was smashed and someone had painted "We hate Arabs" and "Move or we'll get you" on the sidewalk.

The Warahs reluctantly decided to heed the warning and have rented an apartment in Wayne [another Detroit-area community].

Former U.S. Senator James Abourezk, who founded the American-Arab Anti-Discrimination Committee (ADC), told reporter Hundley that in 1986 anti-Arab incidents ranged "from bomb scares and threatening phone calls to the murder in a Philadelphia suburb of a prominent Arab American university professor." The year before, a regional director for ADC was killed when a bomb exploded in his office, and bombings and arson were reported in other cities.

Violence against American Arabs is matched by violence against Asian immigrants and American citizens of Asian descent—Chinese, Japanese, Vietnamese, Cambodians, Laotians, and Filipinos. Attacks against Asian Americans have taken place across the nation from New York to California, from Michigan to Texas. The incidents in recent years have involved harassment, beatings, abduction, rape, and murder.

A recent case involved Felizardo Villarino, who grew up in the Philippines, was educated at the Harvard School of Public Health, and settled in the affluent Boston suburb of Wellesley, Massachusetts, in 1984. Not long after Villarino bought a seven-room home with a carriage house, he was told by neighbors, elderly Mary Rutledge and her middle-aged sons, that he had no business living in the area next to "blue bloods in New England."

When Villarino decided to rent his home to foreign students and renovate the carriage house for his own living quarters, the Rutledges became more vicious, throwing rocks and bags of human feces at him. The Rutledges threatened to blow

Villarino's head off if he didn't "stop bringing niggers from India and niggers from Africa" and Hispanics into the neighborhood.

In December 1987, Villarino finally went to court. The state attorney general ordered the Rutledges to stop harassing Villarino or face fines and prison sentences.

Another case of harassment led to extreme violence. Vincent Chin, a young man of Chinese ancestry, was having a drink at a bar in Detroit, Michigan, when Ronald Ebens, a laid-off auto worker and his stepfather, who also were drinking, began to harass Chin. Ebens believed Chin was Japanese and blamed him for unemployment in the American auto industry— caused, the men said, by Japanese car imports. After Chin left the bar, Ebans and his stepfather went hunting for him. Ebens found Chin in a parking lot and attacked and beat him with a baseball bat. Chin died four days later. Ebens was charged with manslaughter and was convicted, but a federal appeals court reversed the conviction, ordering a new trial.

Not all anti-Asian acts can be blamed on white America, however. During the 1980s, there has been an increasing number of incidents of black harassment of Asians living in the low-income centers of such cities as Los Angeles, Philadelphia, New York, and Washington, D.C. According to reports in major newspapers and magazines, black Americans have threatened or attacked Asian Americans or vandalized Asian-American stores and shops that are located in predominantly black neighborhoods. In one instance in Washington, D.C., black residents boycotted a Chinese American food shop, hoping to close it down because of fears that Asians would take over businesses in the neighborhood.

Anti-Asian feelings among some blacks in inner-city neighborhoods appear to be rooted in the belief that members of another ethnic group may succeed at the expense of poor blacks. Asian American stores owners usually run their businesses with members of their own families, who are unpaid. As a result, families may be able to work their way out of poverty fairly quickly, then move out of the area to a more affluent neighborhood. Since blacks have not been able to move out of poor neighborhoods as quickly as Asian Americans, resentment and anger grow as blacks continue to feel exploited.

No matter which group is the object of hatred, bigoted and racist acts take many forms. Sometimes an individual seems to store up prejudice and then release it when there appears to be a convenient victim. One such incident took place in a small northern Indiana community where John, a young man of mixed ancestry, was working in a Montgomery Ward credit department. He was attempting to deal with a middle-aged white woman who had a complaint about her bill. Since the computer in the department had shut down, John explained politely that he was sorry there was little he could do to solve the woman's problem at the moment, but she could return at a later time.

Continuing to demand action, the customer paced back and forth in front of the counter, then screeched at John, "Get your black ass back there and get the manager you nigger bastard you!" Before the manager arrived, the woman turned to face John once more. "You half-breed!" she snarled, and she spat on him.

Individual acts of bigotry and racism have also taken place on college campuses, which once were the centers for civil rights action. From across the nation have come these reports:

•At Smith College in Massachusetts the minority cultural center was defaced with the ugly phrases "Niggers, Chinks and Spics stop your complaining" and "Niggers go home."

•At the University of Oregon in Eugene, a gang of men surrounded and held captive a group of homosexuals who were watching a movie during Gay Pride Week.

•At the Philadelphia College of Textiles and Science, Swastikas were painted on a school building.

•At Penn State University, fliers with a coiled white snake and the words "Don't tread on me, blackie" were circulated around campus.

•At Purdue University in West Lafayette, Indiana, a cross was burned on the lawn of the Black Cultural Center and a counselor found the words "Death Nigger" carved into her door.

•At Drew University in Madison, New Jersey, racial slurs have been written on the doors of black students' rooms at least once a semester.

•At the Citadel, a military school in South Carolina, white students wearing sheets burned a cross in the room of a black cadet, who left the college.

•At the University of Michigan, a student radio station broadcast crude, racist jokes. Some black students reported that whites walk to the other side of the street rather than pass by the blacks and in other instances shout racial slurs at them. Racist fliers have been distributed saying that blacks "don't belong in classrooms, they belong hanging from trees."

According to Professor Walter Allen, sociologist, at the University of Michigan, four out of five blacks experience some type of racial discrimination during their time on the Michigan campus. The problem is compounded by the fact that what happens at the University of Michigan—one of the largest public schools in the nation and known for its liberal views and social concerns—often ripples out to other campuses.

Yet the ripple effect does not explain fully why some college students blatantly express their bigotry and racism. Over competitiveness may be partially to blame. Some students believe that the only way to advance their careers is to walk over others or push them aside. A competitive atmosphere promotes racial tension, some university officials believe.

Another reason for increased racism and bigoted acts on campuses may be the growing grassroots view that people of color are gaining more benefits than the white majority. The perception has no foundation in fact but has led to a backlash and a neglect of civil rights policies.

The fact is that "racism on campus is not an isolated phenomenon; it is part of the sickness that suffuses our society." This opinion was expressed in a June 1988 issue of *The Progressive.* The commentary continued with the view that campus racism is akin to "country-club racism that has been revived and made respectable again by the Reagan Administration and . . . reflects the national disdain for what Rudyard Kipling, the poet of imperialism, called 'lesser breeds.' . . . For better or worse, the campuses are on the culture's cutting edge."

Another factor seems to be that aggressiveness, disrespect, and violence are accepted methods for dealing with conflicts, methods often supported by TV shows, movies, books, and magazines. Unemployment, welfare cuts, high costs of housing and health care, and overall economic insecurity may lead to racist and bigoted acts also.

"We are seeing something very ugly—the negative pattern of behavior that is existing in many communities because of the economic pressures that are pushing American families from the middle to the lower economic class," noted Shirley Chisholm, the first black woman elected to the U.S. House of Representatives and now a professor at Mount Holyoke College in Massachusetts.

During an interview before a 1987 speech in Dallas, Texas, Chisholm told a reporter for the *Dallas Times Herald* that people "seek out scapegoats to blame for what is happening to them." Chisholm also criticized federal officials for not condemning racist and bigoted acts. "If you don't get the signal from the leaders of the national government that this is wrong, it gives the enemies of freedom tacit approval," she told reporters.

However, William Bradford Reynolds, who headed the civil rights division of the Justice Department during Reagan's administration, declared that more civil rights cases were prosecuted during the two Reagan terms than during any other period. Reynolds claimed that no data supported a nationwide rise in racist and bigoted acts.

Some public officials have argued that racism is on the wane because more and more people of color are achieving status in politics, as is evident in selections such as that of Ronald Brown to head the National Democratic party. Brown was selected in early 1989 and is the first black to head a major political party.

Whether evidence can be gathered to prove or disprove that bigotry and racism are on the rise, the fact is that many Americans are concerned about the issue. During the past few years, major newpapers have published the findings of surveys and interviews with citizens who have been asked to comment on racism, bigotry, and prejudice in the nation. The *Los Angeles Times*, for example, found in a February 1989 telephone poll that 62 percent of the 400 Vietnamese citizens surveyed in Orange County felt they faced "a lot" or "some" prejudice.

A survey published two years earlier in *USA Today*, a nationally distributed newpaper, included a number of comments indicating the interviewees perceived an increase in racism. One New Yorker, a black man, reported that a "white acquaintance" told him "if slavery were ever re-established, he [the white acquaintance] wanted me as a slave. That shows that racism has been simmering for a long time; people are just starting to openly express their feelings about it."

Other citizens have expressed their views by writing letters to editors of their local newspapers. A high school student in South Bend, Indiana, writing for an opinion column, put it this way:

> I thought racial prejudice was nearly dead in this day and age—something only a few narrow-minded people kept alive. I guess I simply hadn't paid much attention to it . . . . However, my eyes have been opened to the problem. With recent news of racial protest, the issue is very difficult to overlook . . . .
>
> Who can argue the point that what a person really is, is what he has on the inside? Thoughts, feelings, attitudes—these are what make a person what he is.
>
> How can people continue to judge by color?

The fact is that people do continue to judge by color and by religious affiliation, gender, economic status, and many other discriminatory criteria. As one high school girl pointed out:

> Usually my dad is pretty objective—he's a doctor and I didn't think he judged people by skin color or whatever. But one day I was working on a social studies project with a friend—a black guy—at my home. My dad had a fit because no one else was in the house—my mom hadn't come home from school yet—she teaches. I felt my dad got bent out of shape because my friend was black. Later Dad said he didn't want me in the house alone with any guy, but he admitted that he figured the "black guy's hormones might overwork." Now, is that prejudice, or what?

Recognizing a judgment based on a stereotype is part of the process of learning to overcome or reduce prejudicial attitudes. Another part of the process is to look closely at the way everyday use of the language helps fuel racism and bigotry.

Words and symbols can be powerful forces in keeping bigotry and racism alive.

8

The Language of Bigotry and Racism

One of the most powerful forces in keeping prejudice alive is language—words and how they are used. Words shape thought; they can be used as propaganda and to spread opinions or beliefs. Words can intimidate or frighten, or be direct threats of violence. More than anything else, words reinforce stereotypes and perpetuate racism and bigotry.

Color symbolism, for example, is very much a part of U.S. culture. The word *white,* or whiteness as a concept, usually symbolizes a positive quality, while *black* or blackness connotes a negative. Just take a quick look through a thesaurus or dictionary and you will find such terms as *blacklist, blackmail, black deeds, black sheep, black mark,* and so on—all linked to unfavorable images. Many more such terms subtly but unmistakably put across the idea that "black is bad." On the other hand, whiteness is more often associated with positives such as "purity" and "cleanliness."

Since white Protestant Anglo-Saxons are the dominant group in the United States, many forms of expression have their roots in WASP myths or prejudicial ideas about groups of people. Take a look at history books that describe various groups. Writers have used "loaded" words to distort or to justify conquests of Native Americans, for example. If whites won battles, they have been called victories; if Native Americans won battles, they have been called "massacres" by "savages" rather than, say, "a battle to defend homelands."

Many old sayings are based on prejudicial notions. The stereotyped image of Jews as "cheap" and always ready to bargain or cheat others has resulted in a derogatory saying: "Jewing down" (meaning getting the price down). Or the mistaken view that a black person's skin always glistens has brought about the insulting comparison "Shines like a nigger's heel." Or a person might label someone "drunk as an Irishman," using this as a putdown based on a stereotype of a whole group of people. Certainly, some people of Irish ancestry may drink to excess, but many others do not.

Such expressions have become so much a part of U.S. culture that people who use the sayings seldom give a second thought to how they offend those who are stereotyped. Sometimes ignorance and insensitivity prompt a person to use racial or ethic slurs. Take the case of the former governor of Arizona, Evan Mecham, who in 1987 publicly called black people "pickaninnies." He defended this insulting term, which relates back to the "Sambo" images, as simply a "friendly nickname."

Because he was a public official, Mecham's use of the term made it appear acceptable or appropriate. However, there was a public outcry against Mecham and the incident was only one of many that led to a bipartisan movement in the state to impeach the governor. Mecham was removed from office early in 1988.

In a similar manner, presidential candidate Jesse Jackson publicly referred to Jews as "Hymies" and to New York City as

"Hymietown," apparently believing, as did Mecham, that the use of an ethnic label was equivalent to using a harmless nickname. But the term mocks a common Jewish name, Hyman, and the reference to "Hymietown" reflects a belief in the myth that New York City is predominantly Jewish or controlled by Jews. In reality, people from varied cultural backgrounds hold and have held political and economic power in New York City, home for people of many different ethnic and religious backgrounds.

In the same way that racist and ethnic slurs are accepted in some circles as everyday expressions, so racist and ethnic jokes are accepted by some Americans as "harmless humor," commonly shared. Such jokes are based on stereotypes of various groups. One form of stereotyped humor is called "JAP bashing," with *JAP* standing for Jewish American princess. The JAP jokes—along with cartoons, books, cards, and T-shirts that say "BACK OFF BITCH. I'M A JAPBUSTER!"—are based on the stereotype of a young Jewish woman overindulged by her wealthy parents. That stereotype was often the basis for what appeared to be harmless jokes in Jewish communities. But the image now encompasses "any whining, materialistic, small-minded woman," according to a *Newsweek* report by Laura Shapiro.

In many cases. both Jews and non-Jews, men and women, defend the JAP stereotype because it supposedly refers to any obnoxious woman. Although anti-Semitism is frowned upon in many circles, JAP bashing is acceptable in public because, as Shapiro noted, "there's a safe target in the princess part of the stereotype, if not the Jewish part. Misogyny [hatred of women], after all, is even older than anti-Semitism—and, unfortunately, always in fashion."

Jokes can often reflect a type of warped or sick humor. Some that fit in that category are called "Auschwitz jokes."

That is, the anecdotes have to do with the concentration camps where Nazis routinely gassed and incinerated Jews. The tales have become commonplace among some groups in Germany and have circulated widely in the United States. Not only does this type of humor mock human suffering. It also implies that killing people is of no consequence.

Not all ethnic and racial jokes show disregard for human life. But many poke fun at what the "in-group" sees as the "out-group's" backwardness or ignorance. "Polack jokes," for example, disparage people of Polish ancestry and do not take into account the many accomplishments of Poles.

When people want to express negative ideas about any ethnic or racial group, they may replace the ethnic slur "Polack" with other derogatory terms for groups. Along with trying to downgrade a group's intelligence, jokes also ridicule dialects or the way some groups use the language.

Ethnic or racist jokes are no joke to those who feel the stings of insults. One teenager, David Hirsch, who happens to be of black-white ancestry and calls himself "mixed," pointed out that he often has to put up with racist jokes from both white and black schoolmates in a suburban Chicago community. Hirsch explained in a *Chicago Sun-Times* personal opinion news column that when he protests a racist joke, the joke teller may stop telling the story, apologize, and then simply tell it later to another group.

"Many kids will say they aren't racists and that the jokes have no real meaning." Hirsch pointed out. "But what may appear to be harmless can be strong enough to kill . . . . Racism is not only built upon what we learn from friends and what we're taught, but also how we express ourselves in everyday life."

Teenagers Carol Buczek and Donna Houston, of Taunton,

Massachusetts, expressed similar views just before their high school graduation in 1987. Buczek, who happens to be white, found that her high school year book contained a racial slur directed at her because Houston, her best friend since elementary school, happens to be black. According to an Associated Press (AP) wire services story, someone had inserted the label "nigger lover" for Buczek in the section of the yearbook for student biographies.

The slur, perhaps the work of a prankster, appeared in all of the published yearbooks. As the headmaster of the school told the AP reporter, "We have one person who is sick, who has a warped mind and who thought it would be a big joke to use that term under the young lady's name." But the headmaster quickly added, "I am convinced there is no racism in this school or in this community."

Donna Houston, Buczek's friend, disagreed with that assessment. She was quoted as saying, "I have always felt that there was some prejudice in our school. People are so two-faced . . . it's pitiful. It's enough to make me move out of Taunton."

Religious bigotry also is expressed in ways meant to hurt or harass. One experience was described by a young person who worked as a kitchen aide in a Jewish Rehabilitation Center where many patients were survivors of horrible experiments in the concentration camps of Nazi Germany. Some of the patients had "grotesque things done to their throats, lungs, genitals, and minds," the worker said. One day while the aide and a coworker were taking lunch to an upstairs ward, they opened the elevators to find two elderly women wailing hysterically.

The workers did not know what was wrong until they got on the elevator and the doors closed. "We saw a swastika painted in heavy black marker and the words 'We've got you in the ovens again Jew, you thought you could get away but

95

you didn't.' My friend and I scrubbed the door until the paint came off . . . . I still get mad when I think about this incident," the aide said.

Along with using words to insult, disparage, and psychologically try to destroy, the English language is in itself a powerful tool in keeping bigotry and racism alive. A common language is part of what keeps a culture together. But a long-standing controversy in the United States has developed into a heated debate over whether English should be the only language allowed in schools and on official documents.

The conflict goes on in many communities, but it erupted recently in Tornillo, Texas, where there is a large Spanish-speaking, primarily Mexican-born, population. In Tornillo, the superintendent of schools sent letters to Spanish-speaking parents asking them to discipline their children whenever they spoke Spanish at home. At school, youngsters who "slipped" and spoke Spanish were punished. The school superintendent expected parents to do the same.

Spanish leaders in the community condemned such actions, labeling them "repressive and racist." Yet some parents were intimidated by the superintendent's letter, fearing their offspring would suffer, and agreed to punish their children for speaking Spanish. The bottom-line message in all of this? If you speak anything but standard English, you will be considered by the majority of standard English speakers "inferior," "unacceptable," and somehow "wrong."

Ironically, dozens of national reports on the quality of American schools issued during the 1980s urged that students learn at least one other language besides English. But there has been little respect in the United States for those who try to maintain languages learned in their countries of origin. Immigrants are expected to become "Americanized" almost overnight. Non-English-speaking children frequently are put into remedial English classes, which has the effect of labeling them "slow learners." Some education experts believe that in many cases the label sticks and that teachers and administrators then have a tendency to treat students from non-English-speaking families as having less than average intelligence.

On the other hand, some schools in the nation are attempting to go beyond traditional bilingual education, which is designed to teach non-English-speaking students enough English so that they can take part in regular or "mainstream" classes. A new approach is called "dual immersion," or "two-way" bilingual education. In the two-way strategy, students are taught most subjects in two languages. The goal is to help non-English speakers to develop language skills in English as well as in their native languages. In addition, two-way bilingual education involves both English-speaking children and those who have limited use of the language. Students not only have opportunities to learn from each other—they also share the difficulties and satisfactions of learning a second language and usually pull together in a cooperative rather than in a competitive manner.

Still, there are many obstacles to overcome before two-way bilingual education receives widespread support. In fact, traditional bilingual education has been attacked in recent years. Activist groups such as U.S. English and the American Ethnic Coalition frequently criticize bilingual education in schools and would like to ban all official documents such as ballots, drivers' tests, and welfare applications printed in Spanish or other languages. The groups argue that only English should be taught since it is a "ticket to assimilation," or a way for non-English-speaking immigrants to become part of the U.S. mainstream.

A lobbying group called English First is pressing members of Congress to pass an amendment to the U.S. Constitution that would make English the official language of the United States. Although English is the language of common use, it has not been designated the *official* national language. Some states, however, including California and Indiana, have passed laws that declare English to be their states' "official language." In California, there are efforts to ban the publication of a Spanish-language version of the Yellow Pages and to discourage those who advertise in Spanish.

Opponents to the English-as-the-official-language movement say that it is really an English-only drive. Critics warn that making English the official language nationally would only invite trouble and would result in a situation similar to that in the Canadian province of Quebec. For years, laws banned the use of any language except French on official signs in Quebec, a province that has wanted to remain separate from the rest of the English-speaking Canada. Although the law was struck down early in 1987, the idea of keeping a "pure" language sparked bombings and emotional, violent demonstrations.

In the same way, the South African government passed laws that require black students to become more fluent in Afrikaans, the language spoken by white South African descendants of the Dutch. Violent protests against Afrikaans by black students who come from various tribal groups and speak varied languages led to many deaths and injuries.

The drive to get English recognized as the official language in the United States is not new. Benjamin Franklin, for example, wanted to outlaw the use of German because he feared that the immigrants of the late 1700s would "swarm in our settlements and, by herding together, establish their language and manners" rather than adapting to English ways. Franklin asked, "Why should Pennsylvania, founded by the English, become a colony of aliens, who will shortly be so numerous as to germanize us instead of our anglifying them?"

English literacy laws were passed in some states during the late 1800s and early 1900s, when there was a large influx of immigrants. But those laws, which required people to be literate in English in order to become citizens and vote, were found to be unconstitutional.

Today, critics of English-only laws say the primary motives for advocating English an "official" language are fear of immigrants and racial prejudice. One Minnesota senator who has opposed an official English bill in his state noted that such a proposal "is contrary to what we think of as America." Opponents of English-only laws also believe that non-English-speaking immigrants *will* learn English, as immigrants have always done, so that they can be competitive and succeed in the United States. Studies and data clearly show that thousands of immigrants across the United States attend classes to learn English and only a small percentage maintain *just* the language of their country of origin.

The English-only movement also is related to efforts over the past few decades to deal with the nonstandard English dialect known as Black English. In schools, students who use nonstandard English may be labeled "too lazy to learn the 'proper' language." Thus, like non-English speakers, people who use Black English are stereotyped and belittled for not being like the majority.

Thomas Kochman, a communication expert and University of Illinois professor on the Chicago campus, points out that whites often fail to understand spoken Black English and black styles of communication, which leads to labeling black behavior "inferior." Differences in black and white styles of communication, says Dr. Kochman, have prompted whites to view Black English as a collection of mistakes, not a dialect.

Dr. Kochman notes that the style of communication for most whites is often reserved and passive, while many blacks (as well as such cultural groups as Hispanics and Italians) communicate in more involved and expressive ways. For example, many whites believe that it is improper to argue or debate publicly in a loud, aggressive manner. But being restrained is to many blacks a sign of insincerity and weakness. Thus, each group may see the other in a negative light. These different styles can lead to tensions and reinforcement of stereotypes.

However, Kochman and other communication experts, as well as countless Americans from varied cultural backgrounds, recognize that standard English is the accepted form of communication in such areas of U.S. culture as schools and business. In the workplace, for instance, many jobs require the use of standard English. As one black executive in Dallas, Texas, put it: "I demand that people use standard or proper English on the phone and in all types of communication. As far as I'm concerned, that is the businesslike way to do things."

Conflicts over language use are long-standing in still another arena that keeps racism and bigotry alive: classification of individuals by color (race) or ethnic ancestry. Color coding has been a particularly insidious way for whites to maintain dominance over blacks in the United States. Since early in the nation's history, a person with "one drop of black blood" was considered "black" or "Negro." With such logic, it would seem that one drop of white blood would make a person white. But color coding was part of the institution of slavery. Laws passed in the late 1600s were designed to ensure that any child born of a black-white union would become a slave. Male plantation owners who impregnated slave women rarely acknowledged their own offspring even if they appeared white or light tan in color.

Through the nation's history, many states decreed that people with 1/64 or 1/32 or some other fraction of "Negro blood" would be categorized as "colored" or by some other nonwhite label such as "mulatto" to designate mixed parentage. Color-coding laws also included some type of designation for Native Americans. Many Native Americans were categorized as "free people of color" or as "mulattoes" even though they had no mixed ancestry. With the color-coding laws, white officials determined the amount of taxes people were required to pay, barred voting and property rights, and banned interracial marriages.

Although many state color-coding laws have been repealed, Louisiana retained such a law until 1985. At that time, Susan Guillory Phillips, wife of a wealthy businessman, discovered that her birth certificate classified her as "colored" because she was "3/32 black." Louisiana law stated that anyone who had 1/32 or more of "Negro blood" was to be considered "colored." Mrs. Phillips pointed out that she had been "raised white" and thought that her birth certificate should be changed to reflect that fact. Although legally the birth certificate could not be altered, publicity surrounding the case prompted the Louisiana legislature to repeal the color-coding law.

Yet the concept of classifying people by race or ethnic group continues across the United States. If you were applying for a Social Security number, for example, you would see a section for "Race/Ethnic Description" and the instructions to check only one of the categories. Complying with the request is voluntary, but the form points out that the information is used "to find out how Social Security programs affect different groups of people in our Nation. It is also essential for preparing statistics to determine compliance with Federal civil rights laws."

101

The Social Security application lists these five categories for people:

Asian or Pacific Islander
Persons having origins (ancestry) in any of the original peoples of the Far East, Southeast Asia, the Indian subcontinent, or the Pacific Islands. This area includes, for example, China, India, Japan, the Philippine Islands, Korea, Samoa, etc.

Hispanic
Persons of Mexican, Puerto Rican, Cuban, Central or South American, or other Spanish culture or origin (ancestry), regardless of race.

Black or Negro (not Hispanic)
Persons having origins (ancestry) in any of the black racial groups of Africa.

American Indian or Alaskan Native
Persons having origins (ancestry) in any of the original peoples of North America and who maintain cultural identification through tribal affiliation or community recognition.

White (not Hispanic)
Persons having origins (ancestry) in any of the original people of Europe, North Africa, or the Middle East.

If you are of mixed racial/ethnic background, choose the category with which you most closely identify yourself.

Choosing a single racial/ethnic designation can be absurd for people who "identify" with more than one culture, and can raise a number of questions. What about those who did not fit into neat statistical slots? For example, what if individuals are from South America but not of the "Spanish culture"? Are they to be categorized as "Hispanic"? How can a person be "Hispanic" if not of the Spanish culture? Suppose, for example, a person's father is of Italian-black ancestry and mother is of Native American-Irish ancestry. How should the person of such mixed ancestry be classified? By choosing a single classification, a person denies a part of her or his heritage.

The classification scheme has become an issue in the affirmative action debate. In a number of instances people have classified themselves in a minority category in order to obtain benefits. For example, two Chicago policemen who in most instances would have been categorized as Caucasian/white used their grandparents' surnames to claim Hispanic ancestry. The Hispanic classification allows them preferential treatment for promotions.

However, using the classification system for personal gain is not the issue with most people of mixed ancestry, some of whom refuse to assign themselves to a particular category. As Lisa Bonet, who achieved fame on *The Cosby Show,* pointed out when she was asked how she felt about being one of black America's leading spokeswomen, "I'm not black, I'm mixed."

Using the term "mixed" is one way that people of varied ancestry can classify themselves. But finding accurate terminology is no simple matter, as Robert Roberts, Ph.D., a retired professor of anthropology at Roosevelt University in Chicago, well knows. Dr. Roberts, who is interracially married and has researched interracial families for many years, explains that if the term "biracial" is used, it "doesn't tell you what race you are talking about. Some people might think if a Swede marries an Italian, that's biracial. In the 1920s, German, French, Italian were frequently considered races. The term was used very loosely."

Dr. Roberts noted that "the descendants of thousands of African slaves have been absorbed into the white populations in

103

most of Latin America" and thus are not referred to as black. Caucasian, too, is a confusing classification. "Caucasian includes people in India, so you have brown-skinned Caucasians who are a lot darker, on the average, than a mulatto would be. But you wouldn't call them black . . . . Nor would you call them black if they spoke Spanish," he said.

Racial/ethnic classification is a topic that comes up often when interracial/intercultural support groups across the nation meet for discussions and social activities. In late 1988, a national Association of MultiEthnic Americans (AMEA), representing fourteen founding chapters in various parts of the United States, was formed. The new organization plans to work toward eliminating racial/ethnic classifications altogether, or at the very least to reach the point where people can mark, as a matter of preference, their mixed heritage on official documents. Just publicizing the issue and educating the public about multiethnic people also can be helpful, organizers believe, in reducing ethnocentrism and the prejudiced behavior that it produces.

Community groups work with young children in order to stop bigotry before it starts.

9

Group Efforts to Reduce Prejudice

Multiracial or multiethnic groups are just one type of organization working to reduce prejudice in our society. A variety of human relations and civil rights groups—private and public, law enforcement and other government agencies, and individuals—are attempting to not only deal with prejudice but also to prevent ethnoviolence.

At the federal level, the U.S. Civil Rights Commission was established to investigate complaints and to collect and study information on discrimination and denial of rights because of race, color, religion, sex, age, handicap, or national origin. Congress set up the commission in 1957 and also directed it to submit reports of findings and make recommendations to the president and Congress.

In 1983, the commission prepared a lengthy statement on racial and religious bigotry in the nation. After citing a number of instances of ethnoviolence that had taken place just since the beginning of the 1980s, the commission wrote, "Lest the vision of America as a democratic and pluralistic society becomes a nightmare of hatred and divisiveness, we urge a heightened public awareness of the threat to civil rights posed by proponents of racial and religious bigotry."

Of course, awareness by itself does little to solve tensions within a society. So the commission recommended specific steps that needed to be taken "to eradicate racism and prevent violence." These included suggestions to expand educational programs designed to change prejudicial attitudes, to hire more law enforcement officials who are "representative of the racial, ethnic, and religious makeup of the communities they serve," and more intense "prosecution of racially and religiously motivated violence."

Even before the commission's 1983 statement, positive steps were underway in communities across the nation to reduce discrimination and to curb ethnoviolence. Many state, county, and city administrations have set up special agencies to handle complaints from those who claim they have been denied jobs, housing, or access to public places or have been subjected to other discriminatory practices. Usually such an agency is called a Human Relations Commission or Human Rights Commission.

In Louisville and Jefferson County, Kentucky, for example, the work of the Human Relations Commission, as with other commissions across the nation, includes efforts to help neighborhoods in crisis. "Perhaps our most important work . . . has been undertaken quietly [in] neighborhoods where early signs of intolerance have appeared," the commission reported. "In a number of areas, Commission staff members have learned about name-calling and harassment and intervened before such acts escalated to include fire bombings, property damage or physical injury. In some neighborhoods, staff members went door to door offering assistance and assessing tensions; in other areas we did mailings describing problems and encouraging support for the peaceful acceptance of minority people; and in yet other parts of our community, staff members were assisted by neighborhood leaders in building trust and acceptance."

When a Human Relations Commission deals with complaints regarding discrimination in employment, housing, and public facilities, the procedure varies with each case but generally follows a pattern: First, a commission may develop a Human Rights Ordinance that, in brief, says no person shall be denied admission to or equal use and enjoyment of a public accommodation because of race, sex, religion, national origin, age, or disability.

Anyone who believes she or he has been a victim of discrimination may file a complaint with a Human Rights Commission. The commission notifies the individual or company official to whom the complaint is directed and investigates the charges to determine the facts.

When the investigation is completed, the director determines whether there is sufficient evidence to support the claim. If not, the case will be dismissed. If the evidence supports the claim, the complainant may be compensated with back pay, a promotion, job reinstatement, rental of an apartment, credit for a loan, or another award that fits the case.

In Milwaukee, Wisconsin, the city has established a Commission on Community Relations, which Executive Director Bridget Bannon says handles "about 500 complaints from our citizens each year. Some of them regard racial discrimination while others are neighborhood tension matters of a non-racial nature." The commission has also established a program to monitor acts of hate and violence against people because of their race, ethnic origins, religion, or sexual orientation. "To date over 30 organizations including law enforcement agencies have agreed to participate," Bannon says.

One imaginative and effective tool to improve human relations that the Milwaukee commission uses is a coloring/activity book for all ages. Titled *Milwaukee: A Rainbow of Fun,* the book points out both the differences and the commonalities of Milwaukee's citizens, depicts some of the city's major institutions, and shows positive relations between young and old of a variety of races and physical abilities. According to Bannon, the coloring book "is distributed at no charge to schools, churches and individuals and has been very well-received."

City and state governments also have taken steps to reverse discriminatory practices in their law enforcement agencies. In Dallas, Texas, a city long known for its conflict between police and minority neighborhoods, there has been an increase in minority hiring of law enforcement officials. From 1980 to 1986, the number of blacks hired rose from 118 to 282; Hispanics increased from 87 to 131, and female officers nearly doubled from 144 to 282. In addition, more blacks, Hispanics, and women were selected for supervisory positions.

In New York City, Police Commissioner Benjamin Ward has encouraged recruitment and promotion of blacks, Hispanics, and other minorities. The police department also is working with neighborhood groups to establish a variety of programs, including team sports and Double Dutch tournaments, and is spending a lot of time on community relations efforts. The hope is to ease racial tensions and to "put out a few fires before the match gets struck," Ward said.

New York's police department also has developed a well-respected task force that works in cooperation with the FBI to counteract terrorist activities and ethnoviolence. Police departments in a number of cities have followed the New York model or have set up their own special units to collect information about and apprehend people who commit crimes motivated by racist or bigoted beliefs. Task forces or special units also have helped FBI agents break up the leadership of hate/terrorist groups.

In the private sector, voluntary Task Forces on Human

Relations, such as the one in Kootenai County, Idaho, also have developed. The Kootenai County Task Force has become a model for grassroots, community-based efforts to combat racism and religious intolerance.

Because of growing concern about tension between black and Jewish groups, women in Indianapolis, Indiana, have established Dialogue Today, which is dedicated to "rebuilding old coalitions and feelings of mutual respect and trust." The group of forty black women and forty Jewish women explores ethnic myths and stereotypes and a variety of other topics in open dialogue meetings and programs. According to one of its members, Dialogue Today also has developed outreach programs, working on community forums that deal with common black/Jewish concerns and developing an "effective teen dialogue program designed to [help] black and Jewish adolescents . . . overcome barriers to communication and understanding."

On college campuses, a variety of group and committee efforts are underway to create a more hospitable environment for minority students at universities with predominantly white populations. At the University of Notre Dame, for example, Native American and black students say they often feel alienated from campus life and that many white classmates do not accept them as serious students but see them either as "dumb athletes" or as "poor, undereducated, not to be trusted, and violent."

A faculty committee, which spent six months studying minority student life at Notre Dame, issued a report in the fall of 1987 that took special note of the social isolation experienced by blacks and Native Americans on the Notre Dame campus. As the committee report stated:

> The biggest problem is not overt racism but the complacency that arises from the fact that the campus is so homogenous. Day by day, week by week, most whites at Notre Dame have so little

contact with minority students that they do not think of this as a multi-ethnic environment. The dominant majority needs to be educated not to presume that their particular culture is the norm, and it is the majority who must be challenged to insure that this place is a hospitable home for minorities.

To do so, the committee recommended such actions as increasing the number of minority students, faculty, and administrators and creating programs that will help "the majority–faculty, staff, and students alike–to become more sensitive to cultural differences among students and to promote an environment free from any kind of discrimination."

At a number of universities, there are plans or programs to increase minority faculty and enrollment. The University of Wisconsin plans to double its minority faculty and student population by 1993. At the University of Michigan, the stated goal for minority enrollment is 10 percent of the student population.

Activist groups at some universities also are calling for colleges and universities to include as graduation requirements more ethnic studies or classes with an emphasis on Third World societies. As one student at the University of California, Berkeley, wrote in a letter to the *Los Angeles Times*, "This [ethnic studies] is necessary if minorities are to even have a fighting chance against the prevailing ignorances and prejudices many white students have about them."

Along with educational institutions, a variety of privately funded national and state organizations and groups work to educate the public about cultural differences and to promote positive human relations. One of the oldest groups is the Anti-Defamation League of B'nai B'rith (ADL), founded in 1913 when anti-Semitism was blatant. Although organized anti-Semitism has lessened over the years, the ADL's primary purpose today still is to "counter assaults on the safety, status, rights and image of Jews."

112

Through its national and regional offices, ADL also provides a variety of educational materials and programs on the local level to counteract all types of bigotry. One effective prejudice awareness and reduction project designed for community-wide participation is called A World of Difference (AWOD). According to Frances Sonnenschein, director of ADL's National Education Department, AWOD is a year-long project sponsored by a three-way partnership.

Sonnenschein explained that the ADL "with the assistance of other civil/human rights organizations creates localized teacher training and study guide materials; a network affiliate television station provides a million dollars or more in on-air time and services . . . and a local business provides underwriting to cover the project's out-of-pocket costs." The project centers around study guides and other education materials on prejudice reduction that are distributed free to local public and private schools. In alliance with other civil/human rights organizations in a community, ADL conducts "intensive teacher sensitization" workshops, while the local TV station "reinforces the educational component by airing specially produced programs and public service announcements on prejudice reduction over the course of a year."

The American Civil Liberties Union (ACLU) is another organization that has long worked for individual rights. As the ACLU points out, people understand the democratic principle of a representative government selected by the majority in the United States. But even a democratic majority must be limited to ensure individual rights. It is the ACLU belief that abuses of government power and violation of a person's rights can erode or destroy liberty for all people. Thus the ACLU through its national and regional offices works to protect personal liberties.

The National Association for the Advancement of Colored People (NAACP) is perhaps the oldest civil rights organization.

Founded in 1909, the organization has had a broad agenda, working, for example, to gain voting rights for blacks and to end job discrimination and segregation in the military. Such efforts have often involved lawsuits, and since its early days, court cases have been an important part of NAACP work.

Although the NAACP founded a legal arm in the 1940s, a separate organization known as the NAACP Legal Defense and Educational Fund (LDF) has been operating since the 1950s. The LDF has been actively involved in cases that have challenged discrimination in housing, employment, health care, and criminal justice and in suits to win voting rights and to desegregate schools.

School desegregation and quality education have been of special concern to the LDF during the 1980s. Integrated schools help ensure equal educational opportunities for black Americans, prepare students to live in the larger community, and open up opportunities to minority students. "School desegregation cases are often the only way to compel otherwise unresponsive school boards and institutions to take the interests of black children into account," the LDF believes.

In one case, the LDF won a lawsuit that required Kansas City, Missouri, to promote desegregation and to upgrade its inner-city public school system, which had been deteriorating for at least twenty years. The court ordered the school board to spend more than $300 million to bring the inner-city schools that serve primarily minority students up to the same level as those in mostly white suburban districts. The school district must hire more teachers, create magnet schools and after-school programs, and upgrade libraries, laboratories, and other facilities.

The LDF also has been arguing cases that involve attempts by public school districts to resegregate schools after years of desegregation. According to LDF reports, a school district that has once carried out court-ordered desegregation can end their busing plans and recreate neighborhood schools. This means that because of housing patterns students are again segregated. Such action "comes at a time when opposition to school busing is actually decreasing," the LDF noted.

Since the beginning of the 1980s, LDF has helped establish other organizations that work to protect civil liberties. Those organizations include legal defense and education funds established by such groups as Mexican Americans, Puerto Ricans, and Asian Americans.

Another organization set up to protect the rights of a minority group is the American-Arab Anti-Discrimination Committee (ADC). According to ADC President Abdeen Jabara, American Arabs not only face discrimination, harassment, and sometimes violence because of their ancestry but also are excluded from studies, discussions, and reports that deal with these matters.

Through ADC, Arab Americans can protest stereotypes of and slurs against Arabs and Arab Americans in the media and school curricula. The organization works to eliminate discrimination against Arab Americans in the workplace, in schools, and in political life.

Other antidefamation groups, such as the Polish-American Guardian Society, also work to protect their members from slurs and false images. The Chicago-based group protests media images and the "Polack jokes" that depict Polish people as "stupid" and "backward." Such stereotypes have become so ingrained in U.S. culture that Americans of Polish descent are subjected to scorn and ridicule, which in turn can have a negative effect on job placement and political power.

On an international scale, the International Committee of Educators to Combat Racism, Anti-Semitism, and Apartheid has been active for more than a decade. Made up of educators from teachers' organizations that represent nations around the world, the committee encourages the use of programs that combat discrimination in school and society as a whole.

Other international organizations work to protect human rights. A well-known example is Amnesty International. The International Secretariat for Amnesty is based in London, but affiliate groups have been set up for 140 countries. Amnesty's main thrust is to "adopt" prisoners of conscience, those who have been jailed because of their beliefs but have not advocated or used violence. Many prisoners of conscience are held in inhumane conditions and subjected to horrible torture. Amnesty does extensive and thorough research on a prisoner before recommending the person for "adoption." Members of Amnesty then organize letter-writing campaigns and sometimes public protests to press government leaders to release political prisoners or to ensure their fair and prompt trial.

Amnesty, like other pressure groups, depends on individual volunteers to carry out its campaign to protect basic human rights. One person's letter, one person's protest, combined with the individual acts of others creates a powerful force for change. That concept is fundamental in many civil rights and human relations efforts in the United States.

To reduce prejudice and to protect our pluralistic society, organized group activities, legal efforts of civil rights organizations, more equitable law enforcement, and better educational programs are essential. But any group activity must begin with individuals. The experts in human relations say all of us can learn how to take individual actions that break down walls of prejudice, bigotry, and racism.

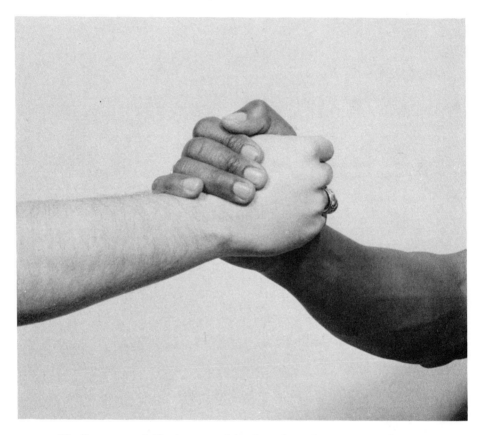

To live peacefully in a multicultural society, we need to understand what we have in common and to respect our differences.

10

Making a Difference

Reducing prejudice usually begins with personal attitudes, exploring how one feels toward people who appear different or act in a different way from oneself. People who have low self-esteem and feel threatened by difference or who need the security of group acceptance may have problems appreciating differences—whether those differences are in color, religion, gender, income, physical shape, size, and abilities, or mental capacity.

A person with a strong sense of self-worth is probably well aware that each of us is unique in her or his own way. At the same time, all people have similar basic physical and emotional needs. To live peacefully in a multicultural society, we need to understand our commonalities as well as learn about and respect different lifestyles and traditions. It also helps to have empathy, or to be able to "walk in another's shoes."

One widely publicized project that helped young students empathize and learn to combat prejudicial attitudes and behaviors was conducted in 1970 in an Iowa elementary school. During the two-day experiment (which was repeated for other classes in following years), the teacher declared on the first day of the exercise that the brown-eyed children in her third-grade class were "superior" and encouraged them to discriminate against their blue-eyed classmates, whom she labeled "inferior." Roles were reversed on the second day. The children soon found out how it feels to experience rejection, hostility, and even hatred, and they also learned that those labeled "superior" seemed to excel in their work and sometimes became arrogant.

The third-grade lesson in discrimination was filmed for an award-winning TV documentary, *The Eye of the Storm*, and is described in a book titled *A Class Divided* by William Peters, who also wrote and produced the TV documentary. A new edition of the book, *A Class Divided, Then and Now*, includes statements by former students, now grown, who expressed their heightened awareness of how racism and bigotry damage people's lives. They also pointed out that the prejudice lesson had taught them to be more tolerant and had helped them to appreciate differences in others.

Another type of experiment in prejudice reduction was developed more recently by Michael Gordon, who founded a nonprofit organization called Innovative Community Enterprises. As part of an exercise to help seventh and eighth graders in New York overcome their prejudices, Gordon conducts a class discussion that involves the use of a rubber football. During the discussion, a student is not allowed to speak unless he or she has the football. Gordon controls the discussion and the ball, deliberately tossing it only to girls at first. It soon becomes apparent that no matter how hard the boys try to get Gordon's attention, he will not allow them to speak. So unfair does the tactic become that tension rises. Some of the boys begin to get angry or show signs of boredom, and a few girls begin to complain. The girls accuse Gordon of discrimination as they begin to identify with the victims (the boys).

After reinforcing the concept that discrimination can create hostility, lack of self-esteem, exploitation, and so on, Gordon then asks students how they could prevent him from discriminating. When he tosses the ball to a girl, she immediately throws it to a boy who wants to talk. The students carry on the discussion among themselves. As the exercise continues, students begin to see that the destructive effects of discrimination can hurt not only the victims but an entire society as well.

Another experiment to help students break down prejudicial barriers was filmed for TV by Westinghouse Broadcasting and Cable and is being shown as a public service program called *Working It Out: Kids and Race.* Under the direction of two consultants in human relations, nine teenagers from Boston area schools participated in a weekend retreat to explore their ideas about racism and prejudice.

Ranging in age from fourteen to eighteen, the young people, who were of black, Hispanic, Caucasian, and Asian ancestries, discovered through a variety of activities and guided discussions that each person had stereotyped images of groups of people. During the first sessions of the three-day retreat, the black, Hispanic, and Asian students pointed out that they felt limited by stereotypes and had to continually strive to be "equal" and "accepted" in a dominant white society. The two white students countered with their belief that all people in the United States have similar opportunities and "if you want something bad enough you will get it." A young man of Irish background felt that all the talk about racism was a "copout thing."

However, in sessions on the second day of the retreat, all nine students took part in a role-playing exercise to learn how it feels to be mistreated because of a particular characteristic or presumed trait. Pasted on each student's forehead was a label that described his or her designated trait, such as "I'm overweight," "I get good grades," "I'm hard of hearing," or "I don't have any friends." Each student was the target of role-play situations and was subjected to the kind of comments and treatment that are accorded to stereotyped people. The young man with the hard-of-hearing label, for example, began to feel that the rest of the group was making fun of him. "Why emphasize I can't hear," he said after the session was completed. "Treat me like you treat someone else."

All students involved said they learned from the exercise that the mistreatment each received was similar to the mistreatment experienced by people because of their religion, color, national background, gender, handicap, or sexual orientation. Reversing their earlier opinions, the two white students said that because of the role-play experience they now believe that people who are stereotyped are forced to work hard to prove themselves. In short, stereotypes were seen as barriers to acceptance within a group and to personal growth and success.

Learning about stereotypes and ingrained prejudices is also part of an Adolescent Prejudice Reduction Conference held in Chicago each spring. Organized jointly by the Chicago Regional Office of the ADL and the Chicago Public Schools Bureau of Social Studies, the conference draws students from inner-city and suburban public and private high schools.

First held in 1984, the conference is designed to foster better intergroup relations by using such techniques as skits produced by school drama clubs that help students identify and define the many forms of prejudice they may witness every day in the school setting. Discussions and workshops during the day deal with ways to change student attitudes. As one participant in the most recent conference noted, "We need to communicate and get to know people before judging them. A lot more meetings like this will help."

"I will be much more aware of my prejudiced views towards any and all people and won't be as fast to pass judgment on anyone," another student wrote on a conference evaluation form.

"Being able to talk with other kids . . . learning what they think about you" was the way another teenager described the positive effects of the conference.

Researchers have found that social contact among varied racial or ethnic groups usually helps to reduce prejudice and stereotypes. That social contact needs to be a positive experience, however—without conflict and with the desire to achieve mutual goals. When people from different backgrounds get to know each other as individuals, they may discover they have interests in common and similar hopes and goals for their lives.

Yet getting to know someone who appears different from one's own group is not always a simple matter. In many parts of the nation, people live or work or go to school in a neighborhood where they share similar backgrounds and are of the same racial or ethnic group. But some school and work settings do allow people from varied backgrounds to meet.

Suppose, for example, you are part of a group of close friends and meet a person whose color or religion and social status differ from yours and your friends'. What if your friends make it clear that they want no part of your newfound acquaintance? Perhaps the group uses negative labels to describe your new friend and insists that "those people" are inferior, not worthy of your time. Your group might even refuse to talk to you if you continue to pursue your new friendship. So you are faced with a choice. Do you give in to the group pressure and exclude a possible new friend from your life? Or do you make your own decision about the people with whom you will associate?

The pressure of a group can weigh heavily on an individual, no matter what a person's age. Most people want to be liked and accepted by peers. But at what price? If you silently go along with the group and its negative behavior patterns, then you give up the opportunity to be true to yourself, to follow your own preferences, and to live by your own values.

Sometimes a person has to make conscious efforts to be involved in learning and leisure activities that include people from other ethnic and racial groups. You might, for example, want to get involved in an exchange program. A church group can find ways to exchange visits with a group from a synagogue or temple. A student group from a predominantly black or Hispanic school might change places with a group from a predominantly white school.

In some cases, bigoted and racist behavior must be confronted in a public forum, particularly if an elected official acts in a prejudiced manner. Such was the case with a northern Indiana councilman, Andy Donis, who created a public outcry when he voted against an AIDS prevention program, saying it was not needed because "the vast majority of AIDS victims are steers, queers and intravenous drug users." Donis's insult prompted protest letters in the opinion columns of local newspapers, calls for the councilman to make a public apology, and criticism from civic leaders, one of whom described the councilman's remarks as "crude, narrow and judgmental."

Writing letters and making telephone calls can be an effective way to voice concerns to state and federal officials, especially legislators, who are considering laws or need to be aware of issues that affect people's civil rights. Human relations groups and antidiscrimination organizations frequently urge members to write letters not only to legislators but also to broadcasters and publishers who present advertising and media images that are offensive.

Many groups provide information on how to voice concerns in an effective way. For instance, the American-Arab Anti-Discrimination Committee distributes a Media Monitoring Guide that explains how to write letters to the editor that are firm, polite, brief, and to the point. A sample letter included in the guide describes a comic strip titled "Bloom County" printed in various newspapers distributed on the East Coast, including *Newsday*. One episode in the comic strip depicted a boy trying to protect his father from the harmful effects of smoking by withholding his parent's cigarettes. The father threatens to sell the boy to the "*)!# Arabs!!" if he does not return the cigarettes. As the letter writer put it:

> Clearly, *Newsday* has provided its readers with stereotyped information about the Arabs. Not only does this imply that Arabs buy and sell children, it also portrays Arabs as people to be greatly feared, which is a serious charge with no basis in fact.
>
> Prejudice has to be learned. "Bloom County" has contributed to teaching it and *Newsday* has joined the rest of the news media and Hollywood movies in misrepresenting and fostering bias against the Arab people . . .
>
> —*Najim A. Jabbar*, East Northport

In another example of protest, Paul Hallisy, an active member of the Biracial Family Network of Chicago, wrote to the program director of WGN-TV to voice his complaint about replays of *The Jeffersons,* which Hallisy felt negatively portrayed interracial family members. He wrote:

> As a member of an interracial family, I must object strenuously to the portrayal of the biracial family on this show. The husband is a passive, moronic boob, the wife is a pretentious witch, and the children are confused and tragic. This is the only interracial family show on TV that I am aware of, but the images projected are so unrepresentative and so reinforcing of negative stereotypes that it would be better not shown at all.

> I also object to the verbal abuse such as "honky" and "zebra" aimed at and about this family. We all know that words like "nigger" or "kike" would never reach the air nowadays, so neither should these other slurs be allowed . . .

Hallisy pointed out that when the show was created, it "was considered very funny . . . . [But] many of us fail to see the humor." As Hallisy noted, viewers frequently accepted television images as legitimate—"if I heard it on TV, it must be OK to say it, right?"—and suggested that the station at least delete the racial epithets or substitute another series with major black characters.

Protest letters and calls can bring results. As an example, a major advertising firm lost its account for the TV show *Dynasty* because of a public uproar over its commercial labeling the three female leads in *Dynasty* "Bitch, Bitch, Bitch." In another instance, a popular Chicago radio personality, Bob Collins, was highly criticized when he described a person of Italian ancestry as a "dago." Collins said he was unaware that the term was insulting and apologized.

In some instances, individuals must go beyond written or oral protests and take legal action in an attempt to stop prejudiced behavior. Take the case of a former police dispatcher, a black woman, in Long Branch, New Jersey. The woman filed a lawsuit against the city, charging that racial and ethnic jokes told by fellow workers were "insulting and demeaning" and caused duress, forcing her to resign.

The court awarded the former city worker damages of $1,500 plus legal costs payable by the city. Because of the court ruling, officials of Long Branch passed an ordinance that prohibits city employees from telling racial or ethnic jokes on the job.

Individual actions against prejudice, bigotry, and racism can

126

be taken on many fronts. Some people may choose to live in integrated neighborhoods in order to be part of a multicultural environment and to have opportunities to know people from diverse backgrounds. In fact, the Urban Institute analyzed census data in 1987 and found that even though many neighborhoods are still highly segregated, a fairly large portion of suburban communities became integrated during the 1980s. Apparently, integration is increasing because of a 1968 law that prohibits discrimination in housing and because more middle-class and affluent minority group members are able to move from inner cities to suburban neighborhoods.

A person also might attempt to combat prejudiced acts by networking—seeking support and help from other individuals concerned about reducing bigotry and racism. A woman living in the Northwest did just that when she found a KKK bumper sticker on her mailbox. The woman first called police but was told that nothing could be done. So she called friends, neighbors, and acquaintances, who in turn contacted the media to protest the police inaction. As the story was publicized, many other citizens wrote or called to also protest the harassment. Later, the officer who failed to respond to the woman's complaint was found "irresponsible" and forced to leave the department.

Students in the United States and around the world often form groups to work on specific projects aimed at overcoming prejudiced behavior. Students also call attention to problems that have come about because of discrimination or neglect of a particular group's needs. In a British school, for example, a group of girls tested whether handicapped people could use public facilities in their city. The girls, all physically able, pushed one of their group in a rented wheelchair to varied businesses and onto local buses. Their experiences proved that handicapped people had to face many barriers as they tried to gain access to buildings and transportation. So the students wrote a critical report that helped publicize the difficulties and bring action to solve the problem.

Many other student activities worldwide have included fund-raising events to help families of political prisoners and marches to protest government policies that deny people their rights such as those in South Africa, in the Soviet Union, and in some Latin American countries. Concerts and street dramas help call attention to civil rights violations, discrimination, bigotry, and racism.

Perhaps one of the most effective measures one person can take is speaking out. To remain silent may be seen as condoning bigoted and racist acts. You can refuse to listen to racist jokes, object to stereotyped labels, or simply say that you are offended by a racist or bigoted remark, whether or not that remark is directed at you.

The value of speaking up was clearly made by a German Lutheran minister, Rev. Martin Niemoeller, who was arrested by the Nazi Gestapo in 1938. Because of his work against the Nazis, Niemoeller was sent to the Dachau concentration camp. After the Allied forces liberated the camp in 1945, Rev. Niemoeller explained why it is so important to speak up. His much-quoted words are as relevant today as they were several decades ago:

> In Germany, the Nazis first came for the communists, and I didn't speak up because I wasn't a communist. Then they came for the Jews, and I didn't speak up because I wasn't a Jew. Then they came for the trade unionists, and I didn't speak up because I wasn't a trade unionist. Then they came for the Catholics, and I didn't speak up because I was a Protestant. Then they came for me, and by that time there was no one left to speak for me.

Notes and References by Chapter

The following source materials will provide further information on topics covered in each chapter. Some reference titles are self-explanatory; others are briefly annotated to aid in further research.

Chapter 1

Allport, Gordon W. *ABC's of Scapegoating.* New York: Anti-Defamation League of B'nai B'rith, 1979.

————*The Nature of Prejudice.* Reading, Mass.: Addison-Wesley, 1987. (First published 1958; the 10th printing of a classic study of the roots of discrimination.)

Byrnes, Deborah A. "Children and Prejudice." *Social Education*, April/May 1988, pp. 265-71. (One of several articles in this issue dealing with ways to reduce prejudice and bigoted acts.)

Council on Interracial Books for Children. *Definitions of Racism.* New York: Council on Interracial Books for Children, 1986. (A brochure with brief examples of various forms of racism.)

Feagin, Joe R., and Feagin, Clairece Booher. *Discrimination American Style: Institutional Racism and Sexism.* Englewood Cliffs, N.J.: Prentice-Hall, 1978.

Glock, Charles Y., and others. *Adolescent Prejudice.* New York: Harper and Row, 1975.

Hosokawa, Bill. *Thirty-five Years in the Frying Pan.* New York: Mc-Graw-Hill, 1978. (A collection of articles from this columnist who wrote about the discrimination against Japanese Americans during World War II.)

"Japanese-Americans Seek Redress From Court." *Congressional Quarterly*, April 18, 1987, pp. 723-26.

Kramer, Michael. "Loud and Clear: Farakhan's Anti-Semitism." *New York*, October 21, 1985, pp. 22-23.

Pascoe, Elaine. *Racial Prejudice.* New York: Franklin Watts, 1985.

Shiman, David A. *The Prejudice Book.* New York: Anti-Defamation League of B'nai B'rith, 1979.

Simpson, George Eaton, and Yinger, J. Milton. *Racial and Cultural Minorities: An Anlaysis of Prejudice and Discrimination.* New York: Harper and Row, 1958.

Van Til, William. *Prejudiced—How Do People Get That Way?* New York: Anti-Defamation League of B'nai B'rith, 1975.

Chapter 2

Alba, Richard D., ed. *Ethnicity and Race in the U.S.A.* New York and London: Routledge, 1985. (A collection of studies on major ethnic and racial groups in the United States. The studies are the result of a conference, "Ethnicity and Race in the Last Quarter of the Twentieth Century," held at the State University of New York in Albany.)

Banton, Michael. *Racial and Ethnic Competition.* Cambridge, London, and New York: Cambridge University Press, 1983. (Comparative history of racial relations in South Africa, the United States, and Britain.)

Campbell, Angus. *White Attitudes Toward Black People.* Ann Arbor, Mich.: Institute for Social Research, University of Michigan, 1971.

Cohen, Robert. Photographs by Ken Heyman. *The Color of Man.* New York: Random House, 1968.

Davis, Lenwood G., ed. *Black-Jewish Relations in the United States.* Westport, Conn: Greenwood, 1984.

Fallows, James. "Asia: Nobody Wants a Melting Pot." *U.S. News & World Report,* June 22, 1987, p. 39.

Furnas, J. C. *The Americans: A Social History of the United States 1587-1914.* New York: G. P. Putnam's Sons, 1969.

Glazer, Nathan. *Ethnic Dilemmas 1964-1982.* Cambridge, and London: Harvard University Press, 1983. (Analysis of racial and ethnic conflict in the United States from 1964 through 1982.)

Goldsby, Richard A. *Race and Races.* New York: Macmillan, 1971.

"The Holocaust in History." *The Record.* (16-page tabloid published by the Anti-Defamation League of B'nai B'rith in cooperation with the National Council for the Social Studies; no date.)

King, James C. *The Biology of Race.* Berkeley and Los Angeles: University of California Press, 1981.

Monroe, Sylvester. "Blacks in Britain: Grim Lives, Grimmer Prospects." *Newsweek* January 4, 1988, pp. 32-33.

Montague, Ashley. *Man's Most Dangerous Myth: The Fallacy of Race.* New York: Oxford University Press, 1974.

————, ed. *Race and IQ.* New York: Oxford University Press, 1975.

Open School students (Johannesburg, South Africa). *Two Dogs and Freedom: Black Children of South Africa Speak Out.* New York: Rossett and Company, 1987. (Essays and pictures by black children show how apartheid affects their lives.)

Powell, Richard R., and Garcia, Jesus." About Stereotypes." *Science and Children,* February 1988, pp. 21-22. (Discusses need to show more female and minority role models in textbook illustrations.)

Steinberg, Stephen. *The Ethnic Myth: Race, Ethnicity, and Class in America.* New York: Atheneum, 1981. (Discusses prejudice and discrimination against various ethnic/racial groups since the colonial period in the United States.)

Tierney, John, with Wright, Lynda, and Springen, Karen. "The Search for Adam and Eve." *Newsweek,* January 11, 1988, pp. 46-52.

Treece, James B. "Nakasone's Ugly Remark Says a Lot About Today's Japan. *Business Week,* October 13, 1986, p. 66.

Chapter 3

Adler, Jerry, with Washington, Frank S. "Cookie Jars of Oppression." *Newsweek,* May 16, 1988, pp. 75-76. (Article describes cookie jars and other collectibles from the past that depict blacks in stereotyped ways.)

Appel, John, and Appel, Selma. "Anti-Semitism in American Caricature." *Society,* November/December, 1986, pp. 78-83.

Associated Press. "CBS Sports Gives Jimmy 'The Greek' the Boot." Various newspaper stories, January 17, 1988.

Boskin, Joseph. *Sambo: The Rise and Demise of an American Jester.* New York and Oxford: Oxford University Press, 1986.

Deutsch, Claudia H. "Still on the Outside Looking In." *The New York Times,* July 5, 1987, Sec. 3 pp. 1+.

Ehrlich, Paul R., and Feldman, S. Shirley. *The Race Bomb* (Chapter 3, "Races in a Social Context"). New York: Quadrangle/The New York Times Book Company, 1977.

Giordano, Joseph. "The Mafia Mystique." *U.S. News & World Report,* February 16, 1987, p. 6. (An opinion piece protesting media stereotypes of people of Italian ancestry.)

Glenbard East Echo Staff. *Teenagers Themselves* (Chapter 12, "Prejudice"). New York: Adama Books, 1984.

Roselini, Lynn, and others. "Strike One and You're Out." *U.S. News & World Report,* July 27, 1987, pp. 52-57. (An article about racism in professional sports.)

Ryan, William. *Blaming the Victim.* Revised Edition. New York: Vintage Books, 1976 (first published 1971).

Shaheen, Jack. "The Influence of the Arab Stereotype on American Children." Special Report, American-Arab Anti-Discrimination Committee. No date.

Sowell, Thomas. *The Economics and Politics of Race: An International Perspective.* New York: William Morrow, 1983.

Stepan, Nancy. *The Idea of Race in Science: Great Britain 1800-1960.* London: The Macmillan Press Ltd./Hamden, Conn.: Archon Books, 1982.

Wellman, David T. *Portraits of White Racism.* Cambridge and New York: Cambridge Univerity Press, 1977.

Chapter 4

"Episodes of Recurring Hatred." *America,* March 23, 1985, p. 225.

Extremist Groups in the United States: A Curriculum Guide. New York: Anti-Defamation League of B'nai B'rith, 1986.

"The Hate Movement Today: A Chronicle of Violence and Disarray." Special Report, Anti-Defamation League of B'nai B'rith, 1987.

Ingalls, Robert P. *Hoods: The Story of the Ku Klux Klan.* New York: G. P. Putnam's Sons, 1979.

"Inquiry: Forsyth County–Racial Questions Divide Residents." *USA Today,* February 19, 1987, p. 11A.

Lee, Martin A., and Coogan, Kevin. "Killers on the Right: Inside Europe's Fascist Underground." *Mother Jones,* May 1987, pp. 41-54.

Leo, John. "A Chilling Wave of Racism." *Time,* January 25, 1988, p. 57.

Proceedings of the First National Conference on Prejudice and Violence in America. Baltimore, Md.: National Institute Against Prejudice and Violence, 1986.

"Racist Radicals Wilt Beneath Public Gaze." *The Spokesman-Review* (Spokane, Washington), Editorial, November 23, 1987.

Scigliano, Eric. "America's Down-Home Racists." *The Nation,* August 30, 1986, pp. 1+.

"Shaved for Battle: Skinheads Target America's Youth." Special Report, Anti-Defamation League of B'nai Brith/Civil Rights Division, November 1987.

Thompson, Morris S. "20,000 March in Georgia." *The Washington Post,* January 15, 1987, p. A1+.

Turner, John, and others. "The Ku Klux Klan: A History of Racism and Violence." Special Report, The Southern Poverty Law Center/Klanwatch Project, 1986.

Chapter 5

Bruno, C. C. "Immigration as Maker and Destroyer of Dreams." *The Humanist,* November/December 1985, pp. 29+.

Churchill, Ward. "American Indian Lands: The Native Ethic Amid Resource Development." *Environment,* July/August 1986.

Dunbar, Leslie W., ed. *Minority Report.* New York: Pantheon Books, 1984. (Collection of essays that discuss issues and economic and social status of various minority groups in the United States.)

Harris, Louis. *Inside America.* New York: Vintage Books, 1987. (A section called "Community" discusses discrimination against women and minorities and efforts of the disabled to find employment.)

Massey, Thomas. "The Wrong Way to Court Ethnics." *The Washington Monthly,* May 1986, pp. 21-26.

Steele, Shelby. "I'm Black, You're White, Who's Innocent?" *Harper's,* June 1988, pp. 45-53. (An essay on the difficulty people have in discussing race.)

Thorpe, Dagmar. "Native American Women Win Historic Land Rights Case." *Ms.,* December 1983, p. 17.

Williams, Juan. *Eyes on the Prize: America's Civil Rights Years, 1954-1965 (A Companion Volume to the PBS Television Series).* New York: Viking Penguin, 1987.

Chapter 6

Bell, Derrick. *And We Are Not Saved: The Elusive Quest for Racial Justice.* New York: Basic Books, 1987.

Beer, William R. "Resolute Ignorance: Social Science and Affirmative Action." *Society,* May/June 1987, pp. 63-69.

Bowie, Norman E., ed. *Equal Opportunity.* Boulder and London: Westview Press, 1988. (A collection of essays on the philosophy and politics of equality.)

Bresler, Robert J. "Affirmative Action and Group Rights: A Threat to Liberty." *USA Today,* January 1986, pp. 6-7.

Cohen, Carl. "Naked Racial Preference." *Commentary,* March 1986, pp. 24-31.

Fineman, Howard, with McDaniel, Ann. "A 'Yes' for Affirmative Action." *Newsweek,* July 14, 1986, p. 74.

Hawkins, Steve L. "Land War: Indian Vs. Indian." *U.S. News & World Report,* July 7, 1986, p. 22.

Jacoby, Tamar, with McDaniel, Ann. "Why Reopen a Closed Case?" *Newsweek,* May 9, 1988, p. 69. (Describes Supreme Court decision to reexamine a civil rights statute that allows racial minorities to sue private parties for discrimination in housing, schools, and jobs.)

Leavy, Walter. "Innocent Man's Eight-Year Prison Ordeal." *Ebony,* March 1987, pp. 88-91.

Louis, Errol T. "Affirmative Reaction." *Black Enterprise,* October 1986, p. 21.

Press, Aric, and McDaniel, Ann. "A Racial Quota for Alabama." *Newsweek,* March 9, 1987, p. 55.

"Respected Family Man Beaten to Death in Texas Jail." *Law Report,* The Southern Poverty Law Center/Klanwatch Project, April 1988.

Salholz, Eloise, and others. "Do Colleges Set Asian Quotas?" *Newsweek,* February 9, 1987, p. 60.

Taylor, Stuart Jr. "High Court Holds 1866 Race-Bias Law Is a Broader Tool." *The New York Times,* May 19, 1987, pp. 1+.

Wright, Bruce. *Black Robes, White Justice: Why Our Justice System Doesn't Work for Blacks.* New York: Lyle Stuart, 1987.

Chapter 7

"The American Press Looks at Arab-Americans." Special Report, American-Arab Anti-Discrimination Committee, September 1987. (A collection of newspaper articles describing prejudice and discrimination against American Arabs.)

"Black and White: How Integrated Is America?" (Special Report). *Newsweek, March 7, 1988, pp. 18-43.*

"The Debate: Racism in the USA." *USA Today,* January 7, 1987, p. 8A.

Johnson, Terry E., and others. "Immigrants: New Victims—A Rising Tide of Violence Hits Asian-Americans." *Newsweek,* May 12, 1986, p. 57.

Kantrowitz, Barbara, with Turque, Bill. "Blacks Protest Campus Racism." *Newsweek,* April 6, 1987, p. 30.

Leavy, Walter. "What's Behind the Resurgence of Racism in America?" *Ebony,* April 1987, pp. 132-39.

McBee, Susanna. "Asian Merchants Find Ghettos Full of Peril." *U.S. News & World Report,* November 24, 1986, pp. 30-31.

Mitgang, Lee, and others. "Wave of Bigotry Stuns Campuses" (several features). *The Fort Wayne Journal-Gazette, March 16, 1987, pp. 1+.*

"On Remote in Forsyth County, GA." Transcript of *The Oprah Winfrey Show,* aired February 9, 1987, WLS-TV, Chicago, Illinois. (Winfrey explored reasons for white supremacists' demonstrations and rock throwing during the first brotherhood march in Forsyth Country, Georgia.)

"Racism in Cap and Gown." *The Progressive,* June 1988, pp. 7-8.

Report of the Committee on Minority Students, University of Notre Dame. Notre Dame, Indiana, 1987.

Zinsmeister, Karl. "Asians: Prejudice From Top and Bottom." *Public Opinion,* July/August, 1987, pp. 8-10+.

Chapter 8

Allen, Irving Lewis. *The Language of Ethnic Conflict.* New York: Columbia University Press, 1983.

"Auschwitz Jokes." *Harper's,* June 1984, pp. 18-19.

Bolinger, Dwight. *Language—The Loaded Weapon.* London and New York: Longman Group Limited, 1980.

Faber, Mary. "English-Only or English-Plus?" *NEA Today,* March 1987, p. 6.

Gold, Deborah L. "2 Languages, One Aim: 'Two-Way' Learning." *Education Week,* January 20, 1988, pp. 7, 24.

Kochman, Thomas. *Black and White Styles in Conflict.* Chicago: University of Chicago Press, 1981.

Lichter, S. Robert, and others. "Prime-Time Prejudice: TV's Images of Blacks and Hispanics." *Public Opinion, July/August, 1987, pp. 13-16.*

Markman, Stephen J. "Classifying the Races." *National Review,* April 5, 1986, pp. 44+.

Moore, Robert B. *Racism in the English Language* (A Lesson Plan and Study Essay). New York: The Council on Interracial Books for Children, 1976, 1985.

Shapiro, Laura. "When Is a Joke Not a Joke?" *Newsweek,* May 23, 1988, p. 79.

Vetterling-Braggin, Mary, ed. *Sexist Language: A Modern Philosophical Analysis.* Totowa, N.J.: Rowman and Littlefield, 1981.

Chapter 9

Much of the information for this chapter came from groups dedicated to reducing prejudice and ethnoviolence. For additional information (or to inquire about educational materials available) contact the human relations and civil rights organizations listed on page 138.

Chapter 10

Banks, James A., ed. *Teaching Ethnic Studies.* Chapter 2, "Racism in America: Imperatives for Teaching Ethnic Studies." Washington, D.C.: National Council for the Social Studies, 1973. (Covers positive ways young people can be taught about the values of various ethnic groups and the nation's cultural pluralism.)

Gabelko, Nina Hersch. "Prejudice Reduction in Secondary Schools." *Social Education,* April/May 1988, pp. 276-79.

———, and Michaelis, John U. *Reducing Adolescent Prejudice.* New York: Teachers College Press, 1981.

"Intimidation and Violence: Racial and Religious Bigotry in America." A Statement of the United States Commission on Civil Rights, Clearinghouse Publication 77, January 1983.

Mustain, Gene. "Students Find 'Prejudice' Appalling." *Daily News,* January 1, 1988, p. 21.

Peters, William. *A Class Divided, Then and Now.* New Haven and London: Yale University Press, 1987. (Original Edition *A Class Divided* published by Doubleday and Company, 1971—describes a lesson in discrimination with a third-grade class divided by brown eyes and blue eyes. The 1987 edition follows up on students involved in the experiment.)

Troop, Naomi. "Black and Jewish Women's Dialogue a Success in Indianapolis." *Forum* (National Institute Against Prejudice and Violence Newsletter), January 1988.

Walsh, Debbie. "Critical Thinking to Reduce Prejudice." *Social Education,* April/May 1988, pp. 280-82.

Additional Resources

Gates, David, with Miller, Mark, and Picker, Lauren. "Lessons in Cruelty." *Newsweek*, May 30, 1988, pp. 54-56. (Describes a museum display that introduces children to the evil side of human history.)

Hawkins, Steve L. "What It Was Like to Fear 'A Knock on the Door.'" *U.S. News & World Report*, January 19, 1987, pp. 24-26.

Hirschkind, Lynn. "The Native American as Noble Savage." *The Humanist*, March/April 1983, pp. 16-18+.

Kleiman, Carol. "Corporate Dress Codes Can Turn Hair-Raising," *Chicago Tribune*, March 28, 1988, p. 6. (Describes job discrimination experienced by black women who wear their hair in neat braids called "corn rows.")

Lowther, William. "Robbing Ancient Graves." *Maclean's*, October 28, 1985, p. 65.

Monroe, Sylvester, and others. "Brothers" (Special Report). *Newsweek*, March 23, 1987, pp. 54-86. (Profiles several black men who grew up in Chicago.)

Rubin, Lillian B. *Quiet Rage: Bernie Goetz in a Time of Madness*. New York: Farrar, Straus & Giroux, 1986.

Selby, David. *Human Rights*. Cambridge, London, New York: Cambridge University Press, 1987.

Totten, Samuel and Kleg, Milton. *Human Rights*. Hillside, N.J.: Enslow Publishers, 1989.

National Human Relations and Civil Rights Organizations: A Selected Listing

American-Arab Anti-Discrimination
Committee
1731 Connecticut Avenue N.W.
Suite 400,
Washington, DC 20009

American Civil Liberties Union
132 West 43rd Street
New York, NY 10036

Amnesty International/USA
322 Eighth Avenue
New York, NY 10001

Anti-Defamation League of B'nai
B'rith
823 United Nations Plaza
New York, NY 10017

Asian-American Legal Defense and
Education Fund
99 Hudson Street
New York, NY 10013

Chinese for Affirmative Action
17 Walter U. Lum Place
San Francisco, CA 94108

Congress of Racial Equality
(CORE)
236 West 116th Street
New York, NY 10026

Indian Rights Association
1505 Race Street
Philadelphia, PA 19102

Klanwatch Project of the Southern
Poverty Law Center
400 Washington Street
Montgomery, AL 36101

Kootenai County Task Force on
Human Relations
P.O. Box 369
Coeur d'Alene, ID 83814

NAACP Legal Defense and Educational Fund, Inc.
99 Hudson Street
New York, NY 10013

National Abortion Rights Action
League
1424 K Street N.W.
Washington, DC 20005

National Association for the Advancement of Colored People
4805 Mt. Hope Drive
Baltimore, MD 21215

The National Gray Panthers
311 South Juniper Street, Suite 601
Philadelphia, PA 19107

National Institute Against Prejudice
& Violence
525 West Redwood Street
Baltimore, MD 21201

National Jewish Community Relations Advisory Council
443 Park Avenue
New York, NY 10016

National Legal Aid and Defender
Association
1625 K Street N.W., Suite 800
Washington, DC 20006

National Organization for Women
(NOW)
1401 New York Avenue N.W., Suite
800
Washington, DC 20005-2102

National Urban League, Inc.
500 East 62nd Street
New York, NY 10021

People for the American Way
1424 16th Street N.W., Suite 601
Washington, DC 20036

Polish-American Guardian Society
6200 West 64th Street
Chicago, IL 60638

Puerto Rican Legal Defense and
Educational Fund
99 Hudson Street, 14th Floor
New York, NY 10013

Index

Carter, President Jimmy, 70
Catholics
    as group, 26, 64
    attacks on, 27, 47, 53, 128
Champanis, Al (former baseball
        manager), 41
Chicanos, 65
Chinese, 21, 22
    in U.S. 27, 28, 35, 82, 83
Chisholm, Shirley (former U.S.
        Representative), 86, 87
Citadel, the, 85
civil rights, 54, 59-65, 68, 86, 87,
        108, 124, 128
    activists/workers, 48, 53, 64, 84
    commissions, 78, 107
    groups, 48, 50, 56, 107, 113, 116
    laws, 47, 61, 62, 64, 70, 71, 75,
        101
    marchers, 49
    movement, 36, 60, 61, 65
Civil War, 45, 46
colored (name/category for blacks),
        59, 60, 63, 101
Congress of Racial Equality
        (CORE), 64, 65

D

Darwin, Charles (evolutionist), 24,
        25
discrimination
    general examples in Britain, 29
    general examples in Canada, 30
    general examples in U.S., 12, 16,
        31, 47, 59, 64, 70, 78,
        116, 120, 121, 127
    investigations of, 107-109
    laws prohibiting, 65, 72, 125
    on college campuses, 112
    reverse discrimination, 71, 73,
    Supreme Court decisions on, 72, 75

discrimination, against
    Arabs, 81, 115
    Asians, 47, 82-84
    blacks, 60, 64, 65, 72, 85, 114
    Germans, 26
    Hispanics, 12, 33, 39, 41, 47, 65,
        72, 77
    Irish, 26, 27
    Jews, 26, 39, 41, 79
    Native Americans, 65
    Poles, 115
    visually impaired, 74
    women 17, 30, 39, 47, 65, 73, 75,
        93, 101
Drew University, 85
dwarfed, 35,
dwarfism, 10

E

English First, 98
Eskimos, 24
ethnic
    bonds, 29
    classification, 100-104
    definition, 23
    groups, 16, 18, 21, 29, 30, 56, 57,
        65, 81, 83, 93, 94, 108, 123
    harmony, 87
    jokes, 93, 94, 126
    neighborhood, 15
    slurs, 34, 92, 93
    stereotypes, 35, 111
    studies, 112
    violence, 54, 109
ethnocentrism, 21, 22, 26-28, 104
ethnoviolence, 56, 57, 77, 78, 81,
        87, 107, 108, 110

F

Farrakhan, Louis (Black Muslim
        leader), 13

organize, 65
stereotypes, 29, 35
Montagu, Ashley (anthropologist),
    22
multiracial/ethnic, 104, 107

N

National Association for the Ad-
    vancement of Colored
    People (NAACP), 15, 60,
    62, 64, 113, 114
National Association of MultiEthnic
    Americans, 104
Native Americans
    classification, 101-103
    in jobs, 70, 71
    stereotypes, 12, 23, 38, 92, 111
    struggle for civil rights, 65
    violence against, 25
Nazi Germany, 95
neo-Nazis, 50-53

O

O'Connor, Justice Sandra 73-75
oil sheiks as stereotype, 37

P

Parks, Rosa (prompted civil rights
    action), 62
Penn State University, 85
People for the American Way, 80
Philadelphia College of Textiles
    and Science, 85
Polish-American Guardian Society,
    115
Polish slurs, 35, 94, 115
prejudice(s). *See also* discrimina-
    tion and various ethnic
    groups
    actions to reduce, 122-127
    defined, 10-11

examples of, 12, 14-18, 22, 26, 27,
    30, 33, 38, 39, 55, 57,
    79, 84, 88, 91, 95, 99,
    104, 107, 112, 113, 116,
    119, 120
Purdue University, 85

Q

Quakers, 63

R

racism
    defined, 15
    in American history, 30
    in Britain, 29
    in Japan, 29
    in Nazi Germany, 28
    in U.S. business, 38, 40
    institutionalized in U.S., 16, 40
    on college campuses, 84-86
    "scientific racism," 23, 25
    struggle against, 59, 74, 78, 108,
        111, 116, 120, 121, 126-128
    sustained in U.S., 38, 45, 77, 87,
        88, 91, 94-96, 100
Reagan, President Ronald, 71, 73,
    74, 81, 86, 87
Rehnquist, Chief Justice William, 72
Robinson, Jackie (first black
    baseball player), 60

S

Sambo as stereotype, 35, 36, 92
scapegoating
    definition, 13
    effects of, 14, 57, 86
skinheads, 50, 51
slavery
    in America, 25, 75
    in Greece, 21
    Know-Nothings split over, 27